More Praise for *Why Teams Win*

"Dr. Miller has really hit on the basic principles of building a successful team. The Nine elements provide the blueprint for all coaches."
—*Mark Messier, Former NHL Star, and Stanley Cup Champion*

"Saul Miller is an expert on building winning teams. As I have learned more and more about Toyota it is clear that the key to their success is building winning teams, from the close-knit board of directors at the top to the working-level team member on the shop floor. The company is a collection of teams that are aligned through a very strong set of common values, a vision of benefitting society at the top, and aligned goals and metrics from top to bottom. This book provides important insights on how you can develop winning teams from top to bottom."
—*Jeffery K. Liker, Professor of Industrial and Operations Engineering, University of Michigan; Author,* The Toyota Way, Toyota Talent, Toyota Culture: The Heart and Soul of the Toyota Way

"In *Why Teams Win* Dr. Miller describes 9 key elements of team success including fundamentals like leadership, commitment, and chemistry. This book is full of excellent information for anyone wanting to build a winning team."
—*Kelly Hrudey, NHL Veteran, Broadcaster, Analyst Hockey Night in Canada*

"In *Why Teams Win*, Dr. Miller generously shares many insights, discoveries, useful tools, and a lifetime of helpful information, distilled from the front lines of many professions."
—*Al Secunda, Author* (Ultimate Tennis, The 15 Second Principle), *Consultant, Musician*

WHY
TEAMS
WIN

KEYS TO SUCCESS IN
BUSINESS, SPORT,
AND BEYOND

DR. SAUL L. MILLER

JB JOSSEY-BASS™

Library and Archives Canada Cataloguing in Publication Data

Miller, Saul, 1942-

    Why teams win : 9 keys to success in business, sport, and beyond / Saul Miller.

Issued also in electronic format.

ISBN 978-0-470-16043-5

    1. Teams in the workplace. 2. Teamwork (Sport). 3. Success. I. Title.

HD66.M54 2009   658.4'022   C2008-907845-4

Production Credits
Cover and interior design: Adrian So
Typesetting: Thomson Digital
Cover photos: Adrian So
Printer: Friesens

Editorial Credits
Editor: Karen Milner
Project Manager: Elizabeth McCurdy

John Wiley & Sons Canada, Ltd.
6045 Freemont Blvd.
Mississauga, Ontario
L5R 4J3

Printed in Canada

1 2 3 4 5 FP 13 12 11 10 09

ENVIRONMENTAL BENEFITS STATEMENT

John Wiley saved the following resources by printing the pages of this book on chlorine free paper made with 100% post-consumer waste.

TREES	WATER	ENERGY	SOLID WASTE	GREENHOUSE GASES
45	16,354	31	2,100	3,940
FULLY GROWN	GALLONS	MILLION BTUs	POUNDS	POUNDS

Calculations based on research by Environmental Defense and the Paper Task Force.
Manufactured at Friesens Corporation

To all those who put their team first

CONTENTS

Acknowledgements   vii
Introduction   1
The Nine Qualities of Winning Teams   11

Chapter 1: A Sense of Purpose: A Meaningful Goal   15
Chapter 2: Talent   25
Chapter 3: Leadership   33
Chapter 4: The Game Plan   49
Chapter 5: Commitment   59
Chapter 6: Feedback   77
Chapter 7: Confidence   95
Chapter 8: Chemistry   107
Chapter 9: Identity   119
Chapter 10: Character and a Winning Formula   131
Chapter 11: Different Teams, Different Demands   157
Chapter 12: Applications and Team Exercises   169

References   191
Bibliography   199
Index   203

ACKNOWLEDGEMENTS

Why Teams Win is all about teamwork, and I was fortunate to have a team of talented individuals whose efforts and ideas helped make the book possible. I wish to acknowledge Karen Milner, Elizabeth McCurdy, Jennifer Smith, and the team at John Wiley and Sons for their vision and editorial support. I also wish to acknowledge Garfield Lindsay Miller and Dr. Laara K. Maxwell, my home team, for their trusted, critical feedback. Garfield's insight and feedback, and his *kaizen* attitude over the past three years, have been invaluable.

Also, much thanks to the following who contributed both personally and indirectly by providing comments, insights, and the opportunity that led to the writing of *Why Teams Win*: Dan Allen, Steve Ballmer, R. Meredith Belbin, Ken Blanchard, D'Arcy Boulton, Bill Bradley, Alan Brahmst, Bev Brown, Michael Campany, Bruce Castoria, Craig Channell, Annemarie Chapman, Richard Church, Brady Clark, Shaun Cloustan, James Co, Matt Cohen, Jim Collins, Kevin Constantine, Geoff Courtnall, Stephen Covey, Marc Crawford, Mark D'Silva, Willie Desjardins, Robert Dirk, Derek Dorsett, John Dowling, Peter Drucker, Team Fenson, Michael Goldberg, Forest Gregg, Glen Hanlon, Bret Hedican, Darby Hendrickson, Clark Higgins, Ken Hitchcock, Larry Huras, Gord Huston, Clark Higgins, Dick Irvin, Phil Jackson, Shiv Jagday, Davey Johnson, Mike Keenan, Robert Keidel, Alan Kerr, Steve Kerr, Bob Knight, Rich Kromm, Nadira Laing, Tom Landry, David Lanphear, Rick Lanz, Greg LeMond, Rick Ley, Jeffery Liker, Vince Lombardi, Ed Lukowich, Morris Lukowich, Bas Lycett, Lorna

MacDougall, Joe MacIlvaine, Sharon MacKay, Len McNealey, John Maxwell, Scott Mellanby, Gary Meredith, Mark Messier, Henry Mintzberg, Mike Moore, Joe Namath, Harry Neale, Andrea Neil, Roger Neilson, Merlin Olsen, Charles Ottewell, Bill Parcells, Sam Perlozzo, Even Pellerud, Bryant Perrier, Jim Poling, Pat Quinn, F. David Radler, Vic Rapp, Joseph Ravitch, Doug Reisborough, Branch Rickey, John Robinson, Gervais Rioux, Cliff Ronning, Bill Russell, Kris Russell, Jerrid Sauer, Johan Sauer, Dave Scatchard, Rodger Schmidt, Don Shula, V.J. Singh, Marshall Starkman, Roger Staubach, Casey Stengel, David Thielen, Joe Thornton, Y.A. Tittle, Barry Trotz, Bruce Tuckman, Bob Tunstead, Bill Walker, Tom Ward, Karen Watson, Tom Webster, Charlie Weis, Dave "Tiger" Williams, David Wolfe, Mitchell Wolfe, Eric Wright, Martin Wright, and Steve Yzerman.

INTRODUCTION

When a group of people come together and dedicate themselves towards a common goal, incredible things are possible.

For over a quarter of a century, I've had the good fortune to work with teams of dedicated individuals . . . all kinds of teams. I've worked with professional sport teams in the National Football League, National Hockey League, Major League Baseball, the National Basketball Association, and with national, Olympic, and collegiate teams in over thirty different sports. While I was consulting with them, these athletes and teams won championships like the World Series and the Stanley Cup, as well as national and conference titles and Olympic medals.

During this time I've also consulted with corporate teams in sales, service, management, and manufacturing in a variety of industries across North America. Some of these groups increased their sales volume 100 percent, some doubled shareholder value, and others not only exceeded profit targets but were repeatedly listed nationally as a top 50 company to work for. I've also run medical and rehab teams in which the focus was helping people regain their health and return to productive life. In every case, the challenge involved helping people work together and perform to the best of their abilities. As such, I find the team experience an exciting and meaningful challenge.

Growing up, I played a lot of team sports. I was fortunate to play for teams that won city championships in high school and a national championship in college, and later to work with elite sport, corporate, and health service teams as a professional. Being part of a winning team is a satisfying and exhilarating experience. People often compare the feeling of winning to sex. Indeed, neuropsychologists tell us that for competitive people winning triggers a release of dopamine, a feel-good hormone and neurotransmitter that creates pleasurable emotions and contributes to the intense sense of satisfaction that winning provides.

Personally, I think being part of a successful team is a spiritual experience. It requires faith, and giving or surrendering something of oneself for the collective good. In so doing one can become part of something greater than oneself, and bond with others doing the same. In making that investment I have found the team experiences I participated in as a player, consultant, and coach to be challenging, enjoyable, and very rewarding.

What sparked the idea of this book was a synchronicity of events over a span of a few weeks. I had been on the road for a month, working with a couple of sport teams. One, the Nashville Predators of the NHL, was battling for a spot in the playoffs. The other, a US Olympic team, was getting ready for the Winter Games. Not surprisingly, my thoughts were charged with recent team experiences and some of the issues and factors that contribute to team success. The process of strengthening qualities like intention, commitment, identity, focus, and mental toughness was very much on my mind. Furthermore, I was just finishing a book, *Hockey Tough: A Winning Mental Game* on the psychological side of sport and had recently defined several factors critical to team success.

While traveling through Chicago on my way home, I ran into Kevin Constantine at O'Hare airport. Kevin is a well-known NHL coach. After clearing security we sat down and had a conversation about team success. I mentioned to Kevin that I was working on a book about winning and discussed with him our impressions as to why teams win. He shared his experience and insights on team success, highlighting the importance of focus, commitment, and preparation . . . all of which reinforced my thinking on the subject.

Immediately on my return to Vancouver, I had a meeting scheduled with Gord Huston, the CEO of Envision Financial, a very successful credit union in the Pacific North West. The organization had recently merged and was dealing with issues relating to identity and culture. In preparation for the meeting I reflected on some core issues as to why organizations and teams in business and sport are successful . . . in effect, why and how teams win. As I organized my thoughts for the meeting, it became increasingly apparent that sport, with its clear and fast bottom line and commitment to continuous improvement, is an excellent performance model for many forms of human endeavor. And that many of the characteristics that contribute to team success in sport are applicable and would be of interest to a wide range of team leaders and players in business—and life.

So I began to write. Yet, as sometimes happens, after a brief inspired beginning, circumstance and seemingly more pressing commitments put the project on hold. A couple of years passed during which my work with sport and corporate teams took me coast to coast across North America, from California to Newfoundland, and abroad, to Switzerland, Italy, Austria, and Norway in Europe; to Korea, Malaysia, and China in Asia; and to South Africa. In that time, I helped sport teams prepare for the Summer and Winter Olympic Games, hockey's Stanley and Memorial Cups, plus a half dozen World Championships and World Cups. At the same time I consulted with a variety of corporate teams helping them improve teamwork, hit sales targets, strengthen team identity, and increase profitability. The consistent enthusiastic response of all these groups to my input on *Why Teams Win* sparked me to resume, in earnest, the challenge of writing this book.

> *People who work together will win, whether it be against complex*
> *football defenses or the problems of modern society.*
> —Vince Lombardi [1]

Today there is a considerable emphasis on winning and on people working together effectively in teams. This is true in business, sport, and life. In this book we are going to explore nine basic reasons or keys that characterize winning teams and successful organizations. These keys touch on the make-up of the team, its talent, leadership, focus, attitude, chemistry, and sense of self. We'll explore each of the nine keys, discuss why they are important, and offer suggestions on how to strengthen them.

Most of us live and work in teams of one sort or another. In reviewing the nine keys, I encourage readers to reflect on their past and present experience with teams and consider what they and their associates can do to enhance both their individual and team's performance in these areas.

Before we begin exploring why teams win, let's define exactly what we mean by the terms *team* and *win*. What is a "team"? And what do we mean by the word "win"?

Over the last quarter century I've asked dozens of groups, "How do you define *team*?" The most common response from people in all walks of life is, "A team is a group of people working together to achieve a common goal." I then explain that while that may be the popular use of the word, the word originally referred to a group of *animals* hitched together pulling in a common direction to a common goal . . . as in the case of a team of horses or a dog team. Expressed in this manner it becomes graphically clear that if one of the horses strays and wanders off course, all the other horses have to pull harder to keep the team in line and enable it to achieve its goal. Or, if one of the dogs falls asleep in its traces, all the other dogs have to work harder to move the team along. And so it is with teams of people.

A team requires a dynamic shared commitment where *everyone makes a difference*. As a team player, what you do either contributes to moving the team in the desired direction, or what you do impedes the group's progress and everyone has to work harder to move you and the rest of the team towards the desired end. In this respect the team challenge is a personal one. And a commitment to enhancing individual performance can enrich both the player's and the team's experience.

> *Alone we can do so little; together we can do so much.*
> —Helen Keller [2]

A team is the embodiment of the concept the whole is greater than the sum of its parts. In *A Brief History of Everything*, Ken Wilber[3] uses water as a metaphor in discussing the evolution of consciousness. He explains that looking at hydrogen and oxygen as two distinct separate elements, one simply wouldn't predict that they would come together to produce something as different from themselves as water. It is the same with teams in which the distinct and separate elements of the players come together to create something that is more complex and more evolved than any of their individual parts. In *Why Teams Win* we will explore the team process and describe the forces that act on and contribute to a collection of individuals evolving into a successful high functioning team.

As for the word *win*, a definition that I believe captures the spirit of winning is, *to win is to gain through effort or struggle*. In the late eighties I was working on a book on high performance. At the time, my son was ten years old and an enthusiastic Little Leaguer. One day he came into the room where I was writing, watched me typing away, then asked what I was doing. I explained I was writing a book. He asked what the title of the book was going to be. I replied that I was thinking of calling it *Winning With Ease*. Hearing the title he immediately shook his head and curled up his nose in displeasure.

"What's wrong?" I asked, "Don't you like that title?"

"No Dad," he said still shaking his head, "it's not right. Everyone knows winning isn't easy. To win you've got to hustle."

Winning isn't easy. The world is becoming more and more competitive.

In sport, competition is intense, with everyone vying for the same prize, and training all year long to achieve it. When Lorenzo Neal, a fifteen-year veteran of the NFL, was asked how he survived the violence and played so effectively over the years, he said, "I train hard in the preseason." Then he paused and said, "Actually there is no preseason."[4] Training is all year long. And as for security and longevity, the word in sport is that you are only as good as your last game, that champions rarely repeat, and relatively successful coaches can be fired if they don't win it all.

In business, all the screws are being tightened. People want things done better, faster, and cheaper. And as corporations compete with businesses from around the globe, many workers are challenged to become online accessible day and night.

The definition of winning as achievement through effort or struggle reflects the challenging process of setting a goal, and then working with determination, diligence, and perseverance in a highly competitive forum to make that goal a reality.

Not everyone is excited by the word *winning*. When I discussed the *Why Teams Win* program with the vice president of human resources of a large energy corporation he surprised me by saying, "We're not interested in winning here. I think the concept is destructive to cooperation and the team-building process." He went on to describe winning in the primordial sense of combatant versus combatant . . . where only one person walks away at the end of the battle.

His experience was clearly very different from mine. I explained that teams compete and win through an integration of talent, focus, and effort. Within the context of a high-performance team, winning is not as much about individuals competing with each other as it is a cooperative synergistic (win-win) process, where team members learn they can accomplish more by working together than they would by creating on their own. Winning is everyone working together and achieving together.

TEAM = *Together Everyone Achieves More*

Davey Johnson is an innovative and successful major leaguer who won the World Series both as a player and manager and was American League manager of the year. Davey once defined the process of winning as follows, "When I say winning, I mean getting the maximum potential out of a group of individuals so that they can accomplish more than anyone thought was possible."[5] Indeed, that's what winning teams are all about.

Microsoft CEO Steve Ballmer also believes competition can produce a win-win. Ballmer has said, "Competition drives everybody to do their very best work, and it's the very best work of competitors that winds up being the very best value to customers."[6]

The synergy of intelligence, energy, talent, and spirit is a phenomenon I've observed again and again with successful teams in sport, business, health care, and the arts . . . and the keys to making it happen are what this book is about.

Parallels . . . Sport and Business

Throughout the book I refer to observations and experiences I've had working with teams in both sport and business. There are similarities between these challenging forums of human expression.

1. Bottom-Line Consciousness

In sport, the bottom line is very clear and fast. You can see in an instant what wins and what loses. The story or the explanation pales next to the score. Excuses are irrelevant. Indeed, Charlie Weis, a four-time Super Bowl winner, entitled his biography, *No Excuses*.[7] In sport, it's the bottom line that matters.

Business is not only driven by the bottom line, it defined the concept. And while it invariably takes longer than today's box-score to assess corporate performance, the corporate season is endless, and with today's sophisticated technological communication, the pressure to perform can be 24/7.

2. A Commitment to Continuous Improvement

In sport and business the status quo is never good enough. What won last season rarely repeats. To win, there needs to be an ongoing commitment to continuous improvement, and an ongoing search for new ideas, new talent, and new systems of delivery.

The intense pressure to win is exemplified by a Nike television commercial that appeared during the Olympics a few years ago. To be an Olympian is a great achievement. To win an Olympic medal is an outstanding accomplishment. Yet Nike's commercial charged, "You don't win silver, you lose gold."

Over the years I have worked with many successful teams who strived to be the best. Whether it was in professional football or hockey or in the telecommunications or pharmaceutical industries, second place was not good enough. The push was and is to be the best. And the push is continuous.

3. Different Strokes for Different Folks

Make sure you're coaching the right game. It's important to note the different team sports (football, baseball, basketball, soccer, and hockey) demand different styles of coaching or leadership to maximize performance. It's the same in business. Different business functions (manufacturing, marketing, human resources, and sales) present different coaching challenges and demand a different coaching emphasis to maximize results.

What is especially relevant is the parallel between certain business functions and certain sports. For example, the way you coach a sales team is different from how you would coach a marketing or human resources group. Similarly, the way to coach winning in baseball is different from how you would coach winning in football or hockey. However, coaching winning in baseball is similar in many respects to how you would effectively manage a sales team. These parallels between effective leadership styles in business and sport are discussed in Chapter 11.

THE NINE QUALITIES OF WINNING TEAMS

Why do teams win? Basically, *winning teams are about people working well together*. Successful teams are comprised of people with purpose, vision, and skill. Winning teams are groups of people who are wisely led, motivated to work hard, work together, and persevere to make something meaningful happen.

In working with over a hundred teams I've consistently observed nine distinct qualities or keys that are present within successful teams. These qualities or keys are at play regardless of the kind of team I am working with (e.g., sport, business, health care, or the arts) and are also somewhat independent of the team's level of development.

THE NINE QUALITIES OF WINNING TEAMS

1. A Sense of Purpose: A Meaningful Goal
2. Talent
3. Leadership
4. Strategy/Plan
5. Commitment
6. Feedback
7. Confidence
8. Chemistry
9. Identity

All of us have some team experience. We live and work with others in teams. As you review these nine qualities of winning teams, take time to reflect on your personal experience. Consider to what extent the team you are currently with, or the teams you have been a part of in the past, incorporate these qualities. And, perhaps most relevant, ask yourself, "What can I and my present team do to enhance performance in each of these nine areas?"

Although the nine keys are presented and discussed in separate chapters, they are interrelated. One quality affects another. As the strength in one key area increases, it strengthens other areas as well. For example, preparation builds confidence and confidence strengthens performance, chemistry, and identity.

We have defined a team as a collection of individuals pulling together in a common direction to a common goal. A constant challenge in the quest for success is the need to balance the needs of the individual with the needs of the team. Both elements must be considered in the development and maintenance of a successful organization. Each chapter has both a group/team and personal component for you to explore.

Our discussion of these nine keys begins with a sense of purpose. That is where great ventures begin. Chapter 1 describes the first key, a meaningful goal. Winning teams are engaged and enrolled by the meaningfulness of their pursuit. In Chapter 2 we look at talent, the human resource that comprises the team. I considered the possibility of leadership, a key that provides vision and direction, preceding the talent factor. However, in the end, I chose to go with talent before leadership. On most teams I have been a part of, leadership inherits and plays on an existing talent pool.

Leadership is discussed in Chapter 3, both the top down leadership provided by coaches or an executive group and core leadership provided from within the rank and file. There is no key that better demonstrates the interconnectedness of the nine keys than leadership. Leadership selects and shapes talent, creates the game plan, provides feedback, and builds confidence, chemistry, and team identity. Chapter 4 explores strategy. That is followed by commitment, in Chapter 5, where we discuss the importance of individuals' "buying in," both their dedication to "paying the price" (doing what is necessary to create the desired end result) and their willingness to subordinate their personal "me" for the "collective "we."

In Chapter 6 we consider the importance of team feedback and personal acknowledgement in shaping winning team behavior. This chapter highlights the challenge of balancing the needs of both the individual and the team for continuing success. Chapter 7 explores confidence and underlines the importance of preparation as well as success in building confidence. Chapter 8 looks at team chemistry, specifically the respect and support that flows between winning team members. Chapter 9 describes the importance of a winning identity, both a winning team identity and a successful personal self-image.

Chapter 10 looks at character, the ABCs of winning, and it compares and contrasts winning and losing teams in regard to the nine keys. Chapter 11, "Different Teams/Different Demands" compares various sports with various business processes and illustrates how leadership style should be varied according to the specific nature of the challenge, as well as the team's stage of development to maximize team performance. Finally, Chapter 12 describes a number of team-building exercises that provide insight and increase team effectiveness.

CHAPTER 1

A SENSE OF PURPOSE: A MEANINGFUL GOAL

Winning teams are inspired by a sense of purpose and work toward a goal that has meaning for them.

Many of the best players operate with a clear, meaningful goal. Many of the best teams invest a great deal of time and energy shaping a purpose and belief that everyone can own.

Healthy people have a natural desire to excel. They want to succeed; they are motivated to contribute to and be a part of something great or something of value. Winning teams present a meaningful opportunity and challenge to their members. Whether it's to win the championship, to be the best, to provide a quality product or a valuable service, or to make a better world, the members of winning teams tend to share a belief that what they do and what they are striving for has meaning or value.

Research has shown that when a person believes he or she is engaged in a meaningful pursuit, it's both energizing and sustaining. A strong sense of purpose generates a kind of "soul power" that nurtures drive and success. Bottom line: people who have a meaningful goal are willing to work harder, persist longer, and endure more . . . and all of these qualities lead to success.

The origins of the word *goal* can be traced back to two Old English roots. The word *gal* suggests the end point of the race. And the word *gaelen* refers to an obstacle, barrier, or hindrance. All of us are performers and many of us have to overcome obstacles and barriers to reach our goals in the competitive world in which we perform.

Winning teams have clear goals and the realization of these goals is payoff. For individual team members the payoff can be anything from a deep sense of accomplishment and the satisfaction of being a part of the best, to fame, fortune, or all of the above. Sitting in the dressing room immediately before an NFL playoff game between the Rams and the Cowboys, some of the Rams players attempted to fire up their teammates by making comments referring to team pride, toughness, and superiority. Then one player pressed another motivational button. He said, "Hey, guys, remember; this game is for forty grand."

I have worked with professional teams where player salaries were in the millions and bonuses for winning were in the tens of thousands—and with elite amateur sport teams where team members received less than a thousandth of that amount for playing, and no bonus at all for winning. A universal driver, with or without monetary reward, is the pride and satisfaction of achievement.

Goals are basic to individual and team success. One of Stephen Covey's seven habits of highly successful people is "Begin with the end in mind."[1] That end goal becomes even more powerful and attainable when it is charged with meaning. People will invest heart and soul in a process they care about. Care is a word of the heart (*coeur* is "heart" in French) and love is one of the most powerful forces on the planet. Love gives and reflects meaning. People who love what they are doing, who love the game, and love the challenge are energized and face the task at hand with more power.

As socially conscious beings, many of us look for an opportunity to dedicate our efforts to something with perceived significance. Working with others towards something we believe in is motivating. When that same opportunity is seen as relatively insignificant and meaningless, enthusiasm and energy diminish, and performance suffers.

I had a phone call from a veteran professional athlete late in the season. His team had just been eliminated from the playoffs and they were playing out the final games of their schedule. During the season he had been plagued by a series of nagging injuries but now that his team was "out of the running," he complained about overwhelming fatigue and pain. "I just don't have the energy or enthusiasm to give 100 percent any more," he said. "I even have trouble concentrating."

I explained that fatigue can sap concentration and enthusiasm. However, it was clear that what he was referring to was more than simply fatigue. The lack of consequence, his perception of the meaninglessness of the remaining games, made it much more difficult for him to "get up"—to perform and do it well.

Since feelings affect thinking and attitude, I worked with his breathing, then with his imagery and self-talk, to help him create a more powerful, positive, relaxed feeling. I then had him recall games when he really excelled. As he reflected on those experiences, I suggested he acknowledge himself for being the consummate professional he was. He felt stronger, more positive, and better able to compete; however, the absence of purpose, of a really meaningful goal, was depleting and limiting.

In contrast, I have observed clients faced with big-money challenges (e.g., making the playoffs, or the Olympics, hitting important targets and deadlines), who tune out fatigue, unresolved personal issues, or illness and injuries and excel, because of the meaningful challenge they are facing.

While working with one of the top-ranked teams in the country, I met with Jerrid, a new addition to the team, and a player who had recently been acquired from another organization that had been struggling. When I asked him how he was adjusting to being a part of this new team, he said, "It's way better. I really like it here."

"How is it better?" I asked. "What's different about being here?"

Without hesitating, Jerrid replied, "Here there's a genuine sense of purpose and possibility. People believe in what we're doing. We're playing for something that counts, something attainable. And I really want to be a part of that."

Healthy people want to excel. They want to feel that what they do and what they are a part of has meaning and makes a difference. Winning teams provide that opportunity. Conversely, when there is a sense that your performance doesn't matter, energy and enthusiasm fade.

John was an inspired, hard-working executive on a fast track up in a successful and rapidly growing banking organization. He saw himself as a highly competent, 100 percent team player. However, he was given a reprimand and moved a step backwards in the corporate hierarchy when a superior perceived him to be too aggressive and overstepping his authority. When we met, it was apparent that the dressing down had caused a shift in John's perception and attitude. He felt unappreciated and treated unfairly by an organization to which he had given everything. The thought that he would no longer be able to realize his goal of being a leader in the company caused him to lose heart and energy. "My assistant manager asked me the other day if I was okay. She said it looked to her like I was just going through the motions. Well, I do my job, but it's hard to give it 100 percent when you feel like you're blocked from above."

I responded to John very much the same way I had to the injured athlete, that as a highly competent professional he was committed to two goals. One was personal: to be the best he could be. And two was to serve the team to the best of his ability. I explained, "That attitude has led to your success to date—and that's the attitude that will ultimately lead to your success in the future. John, that's who you are, and you cannot allow a bump in the road to divert you from your goal." I continued with something I believe to be a core success philosophy: "If your goal is genuinely to be the best you can be, then whatever comes up, you have to use it. If you don't use it, it'll use you." I explained to John that he was letting this recent setback use him and erode his sense of purpose.

Whether someone has a strong internal drive to succeed, or is sparked to action by the team's leadership or by its history of past accomplishment, people motivated to excel by a meaningful goal will invest more of themselves in achieving it.

A few years ago one of the professional sport teams on the West Coast was underachieving, and a reporter asked the head coach if he was doing enough to motivate the team. The coach's reply was, "It's not my job to motivate the team." Not surprisingly, his response raised a few eyebrows. As a prominent sport psychologist in the area, I was asked by the media to comment on the coach's remark. The coach was old school and I understood his frustration with high-priced talent that needed to be enticed, pushed and prodded to perform. However, I strongly disagreed with the idea that it is not the coach's job to motivate the team. The coach is a leader who sets the standard and the stage for the team's performance. And, as I told reporters, "Whether it's in the locker room or the board room, it is the coach's job to inspire and motivate the players." Specifically, a coach, as leader, has the authority and the "response-ability" to open a window of opportunity to what is possible in the mind of the team. He or she must provide the vision to inspire them, to make their challenge meaningful, and to be the best they can be.

As environmental issues become more relevant and social values evolve, many corporate teams are gaining appreciation for both the significance and collective buy-in of their mission or purpose. Some teams are defining meaning with more than a single financial bottom line. A senior executive of a natural food company explained, "There are three things we work towards in this organization. One is profitability. The second is social responsibility. The third is environmental sustainability." He continued, "Winning for us means operating our business so we succeed with regard to all three of these meaningful goals. A great deal more effort and energy is required to make this happen but it's what we believe in and our belief makes the extra effort worthwhile. People want to work here and are prepared to give more of themselves whenever it's required."

Sometimes the challenge facing the group is charged with meaning to all the players involved. Everybody "gets it" and it doesn't take much more to motivate team members as to the importance of what they are working towards. Sometimes the value of the mission is more obscure and it becomes incumbent on management and leadership to define the challenge in a meaningful way and inspire the troops. Indeed, I have been asked on occasion to help management define a meaningful message of purpose that enrolls the rank and file. However, the meaningfulness of the message is not simply something defined by management. Ultimately, it must be heartfelt by the members of the team. Winning teams feel it.

One team I have worked with for several years is the Medicine Hat Tigers of the Western Hockey League. The WHL is arguably the best junior hockey league in the world. And at the time of writing, the Tigers have had one of the best records in the league over the past five years. One of the many reasons for the team's success is the way the head coach, Will Desjardins, communicates meaningful goals to the players. Will believes "You've got to have a dream." At the start of each season, he clearly defines two goals for the team and for the players. One is that they win the championship. And two is that the players sign a professional contract and go on to play professional hockey.

He explains to the players that the more success the team has, the more exposure they will have to the professional scouts, the more attractive they will be as winners, and the more likely it is that they will be signed to a professional contract. These are very meaningful goals to young men who play to win and aspire to become successful professional athletes. And the buy-in is evident in the players' enthusiasm and the team's performance.

Hockey historian and author Dick Irvin[2] mentioned that during the 1970s when the Montreal Canadiens were the winningest team in all of professional sport, Ken Dryden, their goalie at the time, told Irvin that the team didn't start thinking about first place and winning the Stanley Cup half way through the season, like most teams. Instead, the Canadiens' championship focus started the first day of training camp. Glen Sather, the coach of the legendary Edmonton Oilers (and more recently general manager of the New York Rangers) related a similar account. Sather, who played briefly for Montreal in the mid-seventies, told Irvin how impressed he was when the GM and coach both made first place and winning the Cup the subject of their opening talks at training camp. He said he had never heard anything like that with the other teams he had played for, and it was something he took with him to Edmonton when he kick-started the Oilers on their championship run. He related that the goal he instilled from the very start of the season was to win the championship. With a clear sense of direction and talent the Oilers went on to win five Stanley Cups.

Mitch, a marketing executive who has played a part in several organizations, commented, "In business it is often harder to define the meaningfulness of one's role and their contribution to the team's success than it is in sport. In the corporate world there is often not a clear definition of winning that individual players can relate to and affect." He added, "When I worked for Compaq, I asked myself, can I *really* change or impact a $40 billion company? How can I contribute?" Mitch continued, "To help people feel relevant and involved we have to create separate and relevant mission statements for our smaller corporate teams." That task of creating these unit goals, linking them to the grand corporate scheme, and enrolling the team, falls to management.

A major brewery asked me to help their warehousing managers improve the coaching of the rank and file, and assist in transforming the team from one of the poorest performing teams to the "best of class." One challenge in working with the unionized group was a restraint that limited us providing work crews with performance-based incentives. We began by looking at the organization's mission statement, which like many corporate mission statements was simply too complex and conceptual to inspire most of the workers. After some discussion we narrowed the mission statement down to two elements the team said they could truly embrace: first, *kaizen*, a Japanese term meaning a commitment to continuous improvement, and second, *respect*, specifically treating others as you would want to be treated. We related both concepts to specific challenges the team was facing. *Kaizen* and respect for people (employees, customers, and suppliers) has been the cornerstone of The Toyota Way[3] and has contributed to Toyota's becoming one of the world's most successful organizations. Personally, I've found a philosophy of *kaizen* and respect to be a dynamic and inspiring directive applicable to a wide range of teams in business and sport.

Why do we push ourselves to excel? What does being the best mean to you? Notre Dame football coach Charlie Weis relates, "Each of the four Super Bowl rings I have is a symbol that I was part of the best of the best. Why would you set your goals any lower than that? I'm shooting for a national championship every year. Is that realistic? Probably not to anyone except me."[4]

"Having a dream" . . . having a clear sense of purpose and a meaningful goal can help individuals and teams weather the inevitable ups and downs, the road blocks, storms, and disappointments encountered along the way, and remain positive and productive.

It's been said, "It's hard to stop a man who knows what he wants and just keeps coming." The slogan, attributed to the early lawmen of the Wild West, can equally describe an individual or team charged with the significance of their mission. In any field, for any individual, on any team, meaningfulness and a sense of purpose, drives, lifts, and sustains—and successful teams have it.

EVALUATE:

Please consider the following:

Do you have a clear sense of purpose? Can you define it?

What do you want to achieve now . . . and in the future?

What are your long- and short-term goals?

What will achieving these goals mean to you?

What are the goals of the team that you are part of?

Write out your team's purpose or mission statement.

Is this purpose or mission statement important to you personally?

Do you think it's important to your teammates?

Are your team's goals well defined? Are they credible?

Are your team goals and your personal goals compatible or do they conflict?

On a scale of 1–10 please rate how meaningful the team's goals are to you.

1 2 3 4 5 6 7 8 9 10
meaningless   meaningful

What can you can do to make the challenge your team is facing more meaningful to you and your teammates?

CHAPTER 2

TALENT

Winning teams have the right people on board.

To be a good coach and to win you have to have good players.
—John Madden, NFL Championship Coach[1]

You can never have too much talent.

Talent is synonymous with value. In biblical times the word "talent" referred to a unit of weight equal to an amount of silver. Over time it has come to reflect value in terms of the skills, ability, or aptitude a person may possess.

Talent is vital to a winning team. It's the human resource that delivers the mail. The talent may be mature and manifest where all the requisite skill sets and experience necessary to succeed are present and in place. Or, it may be latent, there to be nurtured and developed with good coaching, time, and "game experience."

Winning teams usually possess a combination of maturity and know-how, along with youthful vitality. Youth brings enthusiasm and energy. Maturity brings experience and the understanding to use energy wisely and well, especially under pressure. Teammates affect each other.

Winning teams value veteran winners. These are character individuals who have been successful in the past, who possess a winning mindset, a diligent work ethic, and an ability to perform under pressure that they model for their teammates.

Along with possessing practical, relevant skills, winning talent also incorporates psychological qualities, specifically a functional intelligence, a positive mindset, and a willingness to work together and to adapt and learn. Dr. R. Meredith Belbin, author of *Management Teams*,[2] suggests that the talent equation for the perfect team consists of a combination of players assuming nine key team roles. A team role is a tendency to behave, communicate, and interrelate with others in a particular way. Belbin labels these roles with tags like the team worker, the monitor-evaluator, the implementer, the completer-finisher, the specialist, and the coordinator.

He suggests that no one person can assume all nine roles. Rather, one might possess three strong roles, plus three roles they can manage, and several other roles in which they are lacking. He says, "Nobody's perfect, but a team (with the right combination of personalities and roles) can be."

Not everyone needs to be good at everything for a team to be successful. A mix of roles, personalities, and experience is certainly part of the makeup of the successful teams I've been involved with. Talent must be developed and shaped into a focused, integrated unit to become a high-performance team. As mentioned in the last chapter, one of the challenges facing business and sport teams is that the status quo is never good enough. What won last season rarely repeats. To succeed both individually and collectively there needs to be a commitment to enhance every aspect of performance. A key part of that push to excel is the acquisition and development of high-performing talent.

Something that differentiates the high-achieving teams from the pack is their ability to identify, recruit, and develop talent. Industry leaders (Google, Toyota, Goldman Sachs, General Electric, Nike) like championship sports teams, are aggressive and selective in acquiring and developing superior talent. Recruiting is always an opportunity to consider and reaffirm who we are, where we're going, what will it take to move the team to the next level . . . and how will the new person fit into the team as a whole.

In a conversation with Annemarie Chapman, a specialist in the field of talent sourcing and acquisition with Design Group Staffing, she noted, "Most companies will choose attitude over skill set." She went on to say, "A highly skilled person with a poor attitude can be more destructive to team culture than a person with a great attitude and limited skills. People with a good attitude are coachable . . . and within reason, we can always train skills."

Chapman added, "A team is a dynamic entity. When we talk about talent and recruitment we must consider skill, experience, character . . . as well as the culture we are placing the talent into. Culture can be a real consideration when adding a new person into an existing team. For example, trying to fit an aggressive, sales, 'hunter' type, who has recently come from a highly competitive, 'I oriented' sales environment, into a collaborative team culture that values harmony and flow can be disruptive, disorganizing, and stressful, for both the group and the new team member."

I was discussing the keys to team success with Charles, an avid sports fan and friend. He voiced an opinion that many people share: "It's pretty simple. The team with the best talent wins." I reminded Charles that it is often not that simple. Though talent is a significant factor in team success, talent per se isn't enough to ensure success. Most sport fans are aware of teams loaded with high-priced talent that have underachieved.

Intelligence is an important attribute of talent. When I asked Rich Kromm,[3] a former pro athlete and coach, why teams win, his initial response was also, "because they have the talent." Then after a moment Rich added, "Teams win because they're intelligent . . . because they have talent, and the talent is focused, committed, and able to perform their strategy."

Industrialist Andrew Carnegie also appreciated the integration of talent, focus, and motivation when he said, "Teamwork is the ability to work together toward a common vision . . . the ability to direct individual talent and accomplishment toward an organizational objective."[4] Teams with talent plus the right focus and the willingness to work together succeed.

Teams with talent and a roster of sizable egos, who are more focused on personal rather than team achievement, can interfere with the necessary bonding and blending of individual aptitudes that makes a team successful. This is particularly evident in "flow games" like basketball and hockey, as well as in marketing and product development—where the synergy and success of the group depends on an integrated team effort (see Chapter 11). In these cases, it falls to leadership to establish a context where "the we" is greater than "the me."

Talent is rarely distributed equally amongst team members. However, for a team to be successful, all the horses must pull the wagon. One team I worked with had an abundance of young talent and a superstar as team leader. The "star" had such a powerful persona that everybody deferred to him. ("What does he think?") For many the thinking was, "He can/will do it for us." Actually, a number of the players were intimidated by him. Not surprisingly, the team didn't perform very well. When I observed what was happening, I suggested to both the coaching staff and the star the need to awaken an understanding (amongst the rest of the talent) that the only way the team could succeed was if they collectively stepped forward and exercised more personal responsibility for the team's success. Easier said than done. However, with explanation, encouragement, feedback, and the star's approval, the talent gradually began to take more responsibility and the team began to play with more impact.

Conversely, many of us have seen a group of individuals who appear to lack extraordinary talent manage to come together as a team and exceed expectations. Without superstars, team members are faced with the reality: "I can't rely on anyone special or anyone else. Indeed, it's up to me, and to each one of us, to make it happen." The usual ingredients in these high-achieving groups are an intense work ethic, a game plan that everyone understands and buys into, a surrender of the "me" to the collective "we," and core leaders who model these qualities—plus enough talent to get the job done.

People are key to team success. Sometimes even when two or three of a team's top performers are injured and out of the lineup, the team surprisingly performs better. In part it's because everyone else takes responsibility, focuses on the task at hand, and works harder. When one pro team rallied immediately after losing two of their star players due to a series of injuries, the general manager explained, "The players embraced the opportunity. They took responsibility, adjusted their game accordingly, and raised their level."

While it takes more than talent to win, the old adage that "you can't make a silk purse from a sow's ear" underlines the value of talent. In his book *Good to Great*, Jim Collins describes a handful of remarkable companies that dominated their industries and suggests a key ingredient in all their successes was something as fundamental and common sense as "having the right people on the bus."[5]

Collins noted that most people think decisions are very much about "what." However, his research (he interviewed hundreds of executives) found that the greatest executive decisions were not about "what" but about "who." They were people decisions. Collins, who is also a pioneering mountin climber, asks, who would you want to partner with in a life or death climbing situation? It surely is someone you can count on. As he explains, "Fundamentally the world is uncertain. Decisions are about the future and our place in the future when the future is uncertain. So what is the key thing you can do to prepare for uncertainty?" His answer: "Have the right people with you."[6]

It's the same in sport. When Ken Holland, the general manager of the Detroit Red Wings, the premier team in professional hockey over the past decade, listed nine secrets to the organization's success, number one on his list was "Good People." Holland's philosophy for winning began with "Find the best people you can."[7] In sport and business it's having the right people on the bus. And that sometimes means getting the wrong people off the bus.

I've asked dozens of successful coaches how important talent is to team success. Their consistent response, plain and simple, is talent is vital to team success. Yet many superstars acknowledge that talent is more than just natural ability, and winning is more than just talent. Michael Jordan, a basketball icon and a perennial winner, created the reputation of being a tireless worker. Jordan has said that being a consistent winner and champion requires talent . . . *plus* something more; "Talent wins games, but it's teamwork and intelligence that wins championships."[8]

What is talent? At elite levels, talent is a fusion of natural ability, skill, dedication, and passion that must be developed through intelligent effort and perseverance. Discussing his talent, Lanny Basham, a multiple world champion target shooter and Olympic gold medalist, has said, "Before my first Olympic I practiced five hours a day, five days a week, for *ten* years."[9] Tiger Woods, possibly the best golfer ever, is a remarkable talent. Like Jordan's and Basham's, Woods's talent is a combination of natural ability, practiced skill, and a dedicated winning attitude. He has been quoted as saying, "You can always be better."[10] To that end he has never stopped striving to improve his talent, devoting many hours a day to conditioning and practice and even remaking his swing twice.

Rick Lanz, an NHL veteran, a successful coach, and professional scout, is a man I worked with as a player and coach for almost twenty years. Discussing success, Rick commented, "Winning often starts at the beginning of the season. It starts when the players look at each other and know that the talent is here to have a very successful year. Right then they begin to think, 'This could be something good.' And that belief in themselves and each other can motivate them to work extra hard to make it happen."[11]

Talent is one reason (but not the only reason) why teams win . . . especially when it is motivated and used wisely and well.

EVALUATE:

What would you describe as your personal talents or strengths?

Personally, I believe I have a talent relating to people, understanding their situation; what is required of them to be successful, and then helping them to achieve their goal(s). The basis of my work with teams is coaching. I coach team leaders in their communication and feedback, and I coach team members in integrating their abilities into the team design. Specifically, I have a talent for helping individuals enhance their focus enabling them to feel more positive, powerful, confident, and effective.

What performance areas could you develop to contribute more?

Rate what you perceive to be the level of talent on your team.

1 2 3 4 5 6 7 8 9 10
poor   excellent

Do you believe your team has the talent it needs to realize its goals?

In what areas do you believe your team needs to improve the talent resource?

What needs to be done to improve talent in these areas? (e.g., recruiting, hiring, training)

What suggestion(s) could you offer to improve or grow the level of talent on the team?

Do you believe others in your group understand and appreciate what talents you bring to the team? (See Chapter 12, Exercise 2). Do you understand theirs?

CHAPTER 3

LEADERSHIP

Inspiring leaders model team-first behavior.

The head leads and the body follows.

Many people believe that winning begins with leadership. Indeed, a basic tenet of biological evolution, the cephalo-caudal principle (*cephal* means head, *caudal* means tail), states development proceeds from head to tail. Functionally, the head leads and the body follows. Leadership represents the head of an organization. Winning teams have a good head, with a brain, eye, ear, and a voice for success. The *leadership brain* understands what's required to win. It can select talent, devise a winning strategy, and organize process and players. The *leadership eye* envisions success. It creates a blueprint or image of winning. The *leadership ear* hears "what is," both internally and externally, and shapes and adjusts the team accordingly. An effective leader knows the heart and mind of the team, as well as something of what the competition is doing (or not doing). Leadership also has the *voice* to communicate, motivate, enroll, and direct the team's talent into making the team's vision a reality.

Leadership is an organizing force that brings the individual energies of the group together. It's like a lens, focusing and concentrating these energies into a persistent, positive directional force. Leadership is vital to team success. Indeed, it impacts on the other eight winning team qualities. Leadership can define purpose and inspire and illuminate a meaningful challenge. It can create a plan of action, choose valid performance measures, and provide appropriate feedback. And leadership can select capable talent, nurture a winning chemistry, help strengthen team confidence, and contribute to growing a successful team identity. When leadership is weak or absent, any of these qualities may be affected.

What Makes a Leader Effective?

Clear Focus

It is fundamental to successful leadership. It is a leader's ability to define what he or she wants to create, and then dedicate energy and time to making it happen. Clear focus helps everyone get and stay on track. *Prioritizing* is an expression of clear focus.

In preparing for a coaching seminar with Honda's sales managers, I asked Blake, a senior sales executive, to describe the most important qualities of an effective leader. He said, "A good sales manager, like a good coach has to prioritize. So many things go by a sales manager's desk. To be effective leaders they must decide which things to focus on and attend to."

Clear Communication

One way or another, leaders of winning teams must be able to effectively share their directives, insights, and feedback with the team. Dave Dombrowski, a successful baseball general manager who played a significant role in transforming the Florida Marlins and Detroit Tigers into winning teams, was asked what made Tigers manager Jim Leyland so effective. Dombrowski replied that along with Leyland's considerable knowledge of the game, his success was due to an extraordinary ability to communicate with his players, and to do it with passion.[1]

To communicate effectively one must first listen and understand. Basketball great Bill Russell has said, "Listening is an essential component of success. A team, whether it's a sport team, a business, or a family, cannot function effectively unless everyone is prepared to drop the filters that get in the way of effective listening." He went on to describe Red Auerbach, the coach of the dynasty Boston Celtics, as a great listener and a great leader: "Red's greatest talent was that he was a listener who translated what he heard into effective action."[2]

Attention to Detail

JD, a sportsman who owns and operates a successful real estate business, cited leadership as the key to organizational success. When I asked him to elaborate on just how he saw leadership contributing to team success, he replied, "Successful leaders demand an attention to detail." Thinking it over, I suggested that leadership's motivation to achieve a standard of excellence is what drives their attention to detail. "Absolutely," JD agreed, "effective leaders want it done right."

When Eric Wright, a four-time Super Bowl winner with the San Francisco Forty-Niners (and now a college football coach), reflected on what made the late Bill Walsh, the dean of NFL coaches, so successful, he highlighted Walsh's attention to detail. Wright said, "Coach Walsh always insisted that we do it right . . . and that we practice exactly like we play the game."[3] Walsh's approach is reminiscent of the saying, "The way we do anything is the way we do everything," a practical and exacting leadership philosophy that nurtures both awareness and consistency.

The Ability to Motivate

He or she is able to inspire the team to give their best, even in difficult and challenging circumstances. Earlier, in our discussion of meaningful goals (Chapter 1), I described a coach who said it wasn't his job to motivate the team. I don't agree; a coach has both the authority and the responsibility to open a window of opportunity, to impress on the mind of the team what is possible, and to inspire them to be the best they can be.

Bill Walker, a successful state champion wrestling coach who mentored winners for over thirty years, cites inspirational coaching as a major reason why teams win. According to him, when any team member comes to realize that their leader or coach is more committed to helping the team member excel than to the coachs'own personal success, it lifts the team member's spirit . . . and their performance.[4] This is true for performers of all ages, especially the young.

A leader may have a sound strategy; however, if he or she cannot "sell" the talent on the dream, the plan, or the possibility, performance will suffer.

Joe Namath, the former NFL star quarterback, supposedly said, "To be a leader you have to have people follow you, and nobody wants to follow someone who doesn't know where they're going."[5] And nobody wants to follow someone who won't get you there. It applies in all areas.

I have worked with professional and Olympic athletes who didn't believe their coach's strategy would enable them to succeed. Without that belief there is little chance of success. Similarly, I have consulted with corporate management and marketing teams that didn't believe senior management was aware of or in touch with what was going on in the firm or in the marketplace. When a healthy belief in leadership's competence is absent, players cannot be counted on to follow through or execute under pressure.

In one case a veteran NFL defensive back said, "What he [the coach] is telling me to do goes against everything I have been taught to do my whole career. If I do it and get beat, it's me who looks like a fool, not him. And I'm simply not going to do it." Similarly, a telecommunications marketing person told me, "I'm in a difficult spot. I don't buy into the program at all. However, if I don't get on board I'm done . . . and if we run with it and don't hit the targets it's my head that will be on the chopping block." That kind of negative thinking leads to guarded efforts and lower results. Effective leadership is about instilling belief and confidence amongst team members that the desired end result is possible and this is the way we can and will succeed.

There's a learning curve to effective leadership. Leadership is a skill that is acquired through participation, success, and the occasional painful experience. After his team's disappointing playoff performance, one coach lamented, "I was naïve. All season I went along with the idea that if I would cut the players some slack during the season"—by lowering his standards with regard to level of effort demanded in practice and discipline on and off the field—"they would give me more in the playoffs when the situation really demanded it. In the end it didn't work. I didn't get what I had hoped for. In the future we are going to emphasize preparation and discipline . . . and I'll be considerably less tolerant." It's a painful lesson, but rarely does compromising standards lead to superior performance.

Similarly, an American League baseball manager who took over a team of veteran players that had performed fairly well the previous season described being overly guarded about asserting his influence and style on the group. After the team underachieved, he explained, even though the attitude and work ethic of the team at the start of the season wasn't what he wanted, "out of respect for these veteran players and their record" he was reluctant to appear too aggressive at the beginning of his tenure. He simply hoped that the players would change as the season progressed. About two-thirds of the way through the season he realized that things weren't going to change and the season was slipping away. At that point, however, he didn't want to act too harshly and appear to be panicking, so, he let things be. Predictably, the team failed and the manager was fired.

As a consultant, I prefer to work with teams with strong leadership. Strong positive leadership provides a clear sense of direction and expectation for everyone involved. Competent leadership also has the confidence to see value in a psychology resource that can improve understanding and focus. To that end I have worked with coaches who asked me to talk to their team about specifics such as confidence and intention, and with other coaches who instructed me to talk with them and they would talk to the team. I have also been directed to talk to specific players about some very specific things.

For example, when I worked with the Rams, Bruce Snyder, the running back coach, asked me to talk with Eric Dickerson, the Rams' star running back. Bruce had observed that during the previous season, when Dickerson ran for over 2000 yards, his focus was not on the linebacker immediately in front of him but rather on the defensive back further downfield. He commented that this year however, Eric seemed to be more focused, perhaps too focused, on what was directly in front of him. His question to me was, "Is there something you can do to help Eric shift his focus further down field and see himself past the linebacker and taking on the defensive back?" I developed a program accordingly. Working with strong positive leadership that provides clear directives focuses energy, and focus produces results.

Leaders in business and sport have to be tough-minded visionaries, not "hopers." They must set a standard of performance and excellence from the start. To win, they must demand and model a commitment to excellence that is reflected by all. I discussed winning leadership with DR, who was president of the world's third largest newspaper empire. He said, "One of the most important qualities to running a successful business is the "killer instinct" of leadership. It's the ability of the leader to make the tough and right decision and then follow through, no matter what.. And that killer instinct has to become part of the operational mindset of the team." His words may sound harsh; however, I agree that a leader's ability to be mentally tough and stay focused on what it takes is a key to team success.

One test I frequently use in my work with the teams is the Myers-Briggs Type Indicator (MBTI). The test is useful in understanding communication and learning styles of both leadership and the rank and file. The MBTI looks at four dimensions of personality style. One that is relevant here is the thinking-feeling dimension. Thinking (T) types are more analytic and task-oriented. They look at what is demanded in a situation. In contrast, feeling (F) types are more concerned with how they and others feel. T types can fire people more easily than F types. T types simply say, "Hey, that's the job. They didn't do it. They're fired." F types are inclined to say, "But there must be a reason why they didn't do it." Clearly, the newspaper executive, like the majority of corporate CEOs, scored significantly higher on the T than on the F dimension. Of course, effective leaders can possess qualities of both T and F. However, if they are strong Ts they have to be careful that they are aware of the feelings of team members. If not, they may experience the team tuning them out. If they are strong F types, they must remember to stay on task.

Successful leadership requires sound judgment, knowing when to assert and when to flex. Larry Huras, a successful coach and corporate consultant I have worked with in Europe, has expressed it rather metaphorically. "Coaching is like holding a small bird in your hand. If you squeeze it too hard you will crush its spirit. If you hold it too loosely it will shit in your hand and fly away." Larry goes on to say the agreement he makes with his players is, "I won't squeeze you too hard if you promise not to embarrass us."[6]

Bill Russell, basketball superstar and coach, expressed a similar sentiment when he said that great leaders possess three flexible skills. One is toughness. Two is tenderness. And the third is the ability to know when is the right time to use one or the other. It comes from an integration of head, heart, awareness, and experience.

Psychologists have reported that modeling is one of the most powerful forms of learning. The leader of a winning team can be a model of focus, determination, effort, dedication, and discipline. Tom Landry, a successful leader of teams, has said, "Leadership is a matter of having people look at you and gain confidence by seeing how you react. If you're in control, they're in control."[7]

One team I was brought in to consult with had a great deal of talent but consistently underachieved in the pressure of the playoffs. Working with the team I noticed that the head coach was a volatile, emotional leader who would frequently vent his emotions in tirades directed at his players or the officials. After several players (both veterans and rookies) complained to me about frequent emotional outbursts and profanity directed at them, I shared with the coach that a number of players had commented that his emotional tirades and swearing didn't really help them to play better. Indeed, yelling as a habit rarely inspires, and emotions engendered by fear and anger often have a contractive effect on performance.

The coach's response reflected his commitment. He asked what he could do to have more emotional control. Over the next month, we worked with his breathing, his ability to release tension, and with the concept of "using it" (that is, the pressure of the moment) to focus on the positive, rather than letting it "use him" (with the result being another thoughtless outburst). He exercised more control and the team performed better.

Along with being able to motivate, vision, strategize, prioritize, communicate, and model, a top down or vertical leader must also be able to nurture leadership amongst the rank and file.

Core Leadership

Leadership is a choice you make, not a position you sit in.
—John Maxwell[8]

Leadership on winning teams is not simply the top down guidance provided by the CEO, the GM, head coach, or the senior executive group. In addition to that hierarchical, vertical, and sometimes "virtuoso" form of leadership, winning teams possess strong leadership from within the rank and file. Indeed, successful teams have a core of leaders amongst team members who model a winning mindset, work habits . . . and see to it that their teammates follow. These player-leaders exercise a vital role in motivating and leading their teammates to generate the desired result. Leadership guru John Maxwell, in his book *The 360 Degree Leader* wrote, "Ninety-nine percent of all leadership occurs not from the top but from the middle of the organization." While I'm not sure I agree with the percentages Maxwell cites, the importance of leading from the middle must be underlined and appreciated.

When I asked Ken Hitchcock, a career winning coach, what the key is to a winning team, he replied, "It's leadership, specifically, the leadership of the players 'in the room.'" He added, "If you have the right core group, a team can win without a strong coach—and sometimes win in spite of the coach. However, even a good coach needs the leadership of the athletes in the room to be successful."[9]

I was having lunch with a player who had played on the Stanley Cup champion Dallas Stars. When I asked him about the role of coaching in the Stars' success he said, "Hitch" (head coach Ken Hitchcock, mentioned above) "was really just a guide. Really, some of the veterans, especially Carbo [Guy Carbonneau] ran the team. In addition to star players like Modano, Hull, Hatcher, and Neuendyke, we had these intelligent, experienced veterans like Carbonneau, Keane, Skrudland, and Mueller who set the tone. Often Hitch would say something to the team and then ask, 'What do you think, Carbo?' Or when he left the room Carbo would say, 'OK boys, this is what we're going to do.' Hitch did a good job but the veterans led the team."

I ran the story by Doug Risebrough. Once himself a core leader on a championship team Risebrough has been the general manager of the Minnesota Wild from its inception into the NHL over a dozen years ago. He said, there's no question the core group is vitally important to team success however senior management has the responsibility to choose the right players and to make sure they are all aligned and comfortable with each other.[10]

In sport, captains are the leaders of the rank and file. A captain is someone who understands what it takes to be successful, has the respect of his or her peers, and models the acumen and effort to succeed. On successful teams captains are often seen as individuals their teammates can rely on for motivation and unity. They are "team first." One of the finest descriptions of a winning team captain's philosophy and one I recommend to all my clients was articulated by Stanley Cup winner and Olympic gold medalist Steve Yzerman, who said, "I always try and do what is best for the team."[11]

In business, a variety of executives, supervisors, managers, and lead hands assume a captain's role and are responsible to see that their teams are enrolled and involved in hitting team targets, providing exemplary service, and completing projects on time and on budget. As in sport, the bottom line in corporate team play is a winning result.

A managerial philosophy gaining some popularity is "servant leadership."[12] Servant leadership is described as winning by empowering others rather than suppressing them. It's said to go beyond the leader-first, power-focused, dog-eat-dog, what's in it for me approach to leadership prevalent in the twentieth century.

Sounds sensible and relevant. I'm all for a respectful people-conscious way of "doing what is best for the team." And I totally embrace the concept of winning by making the people around you better. It's a lesson learned by basketball stars like Michael Jordan and Kobe Bryant as they matured and led their teams to successful seasons. However, I have observed that in some efforts to nurture rapport, leadership has pandered to the emotions of the team and lost sight that the bottom line in business and sport is the bottom line. If, as demonstrated by Toyota and others, winning in these changing times can best be accomplished by coaching leaders to be more committed to empowering the people they lead and serve, then we should be more assertive about coaching leaders accordingly.

Leadership can be coached. I have worked with "captain's groups" in business and sport. These are regularly arranged meetings where we encourage selected individuals to take more of a leadership role. These sessions are designed to cultivate the developing leaders' awareness of issues and personalities, and guide them to vision success, exercise more initiative, make team-first decisions, communicate positively and with purpose, and explore optimal ways to motivate and reinforce teammates. Sound judgment is something that comes from an integration of attitude, awareness and experience. It's been said that having a letter (that is, being appointed captain) doesn't make you a leader. And similarly, not being designated as a captain or manager doesn't prevent you from leading. Jack Zenger, a leadership consultant, has similarly noted the contributions corporate players make should not limited to their position. Zenger almost states the obvious when he adds that organizations function well when people's contribution exceeds or matches their formal position . . . and suffer when an individual's contribution falls short of what is expected for that position, especially when that person occupies a position of power and responsibility.[13]

Whether designated or not, core leadership is vital to success. One NHL team I worked with was struggling and the coach was increasingly becoming frustrated and losing control. Coincidentally, the coach and captain of the team had worked together previously on another team that had won the championship. In discussing the current team's struggles I asked the captain if the coach had behaved in as emotional a manner when they won the Stanley Cup several years earlier. "Not at all," he replied. "In that situation we had half a dozen leaders 'in the room' [on the team]. He would just tell us what he wanted and we'd see that it got done."

I have repeatedly seen winning teams possessing a key group of player-leaders that model the leadership message for the rank and file. Indeed, a number of successful executives and coaches I have worked with have described that one of their most valuable functions is to nurture their leadership group into being a positive, effective force within the organization.

Discussing winning and leadership, Gord Huston, the CEO of a successful financial services organization, said, "My job is to find good people interested in moving this organization forward and to develop these people . . . to figure out a way to unleash their potential, and to encourage them or give them permission to act on their best judgment." He went on to say, "Encouragement means to put courage into people. I want to encourage them to try. If they make mistakes, well, that's what learning is about, that's ultimately how confidence grows, and that will make them and the organization better." Then with a smile he added, "Of course, we have to hold people accountable, and occasionally even trade someone to Philadelphia."[14]

Casey Stengel, the legendary and very successful baseball manager of the New York Yankees dynasty of the 1950s, is alleged to have said that on any team a third of the players love you, a third of the players hate you, and a third of the players haven't made up their minds. Casey said the trick to winning is to keep the undecided players away from the ones who hate you.[15] Well, perhaps more accurately, a key to winning is having a core of players who model team-first leadership and are able to influence and enroll the rest of their teammates.

The Personality Mix

Personality plays a significant role in leader-team communication. The interaction of the personality styles of the leader(s) and team members can impact on how messages are transmitted, translated, and played out. There are many ways to consider personality style differences. Something I've found to be effective is to give team members, especially team leaders, a personality-style test. As mentioned, a personality test I frequently use is the Myers-Briggs Type Indicator. In addition to the thinking (T) and feeling (F) dimensions discussed earlier, other dimensions include extroversion (E) and introversion (I); and the more sensory factual, detail-oriented person (S) and the more intuitive, general, probabilities type (N). Then there's the (J) type who prefers routine, works consistently, and follows through, and the more flexible (P) type who enjoys diversity and spontaneity. Testing team members and discussing the results with leadership and with the entire group can lead to greater understanding and respect for individual differences . . . and improved team performance.

For six years I ran an interdisciplinary clinic treating pain and disability. When I took over the organization, I experienced an initial personality clash with a senior executive who ran our employee assistance program. It was a large program looking after 50,000 employees and she did an excellent job managing it. We were very different types. She preferred scheduled meetings with a written agenda of whatever was to be discussed. Contrastingly, I was inclined at times to pop into her office spontaneously to discuss something that had just come to mind or across my desk. I saw her as hypersensitive and standoffish. She perceived me as intrusive and overbearing. With testing it became clear that my extroverted, spontaneous personality style (EP) was clashing with her introverted, more structured controlling style (IJ). When I understood the differences I made more of an effort to structure meetings with advance warning. As she understood my outgoing and spontaneous style, she made the effort to be more tolerant and flexible. Thereafter, we worked together very effectively.

Similarly, I recall consulting with Dave and Rick, two players on the same pro team. Both were stars. Dave was very extroverted and played his best when challenged. Rick was a more sensitive, introverted individual who responded well to reassurance. In the years that I worked with the team I observed two different head coaches interact with these two men. Both players performed well; however, their best results were when the coaches' style matched that of the players. When a more extroverted, in your face coach challenged Dave, he excelled. Rick's performance peaked when a more mild-mannered coach was positive and reassuring with him.

Focusing style is another variable that can differentiate people. Some people have a very narrow focus; with others it's more broad. Some have an internal focus and consistently cue their feelings. Others focus more on externals and are more tuned in to what's going on around them. All these factors play into how messages are communicated and received. I have tested leadership groups and the rank and file to help leaders understand their team members, and, in some cases, to help team members understand leadership. Understanding leads to positive results. Whether one is a leader or not, it's important to understand who you are and to whom you are relating.

Cliff Ronning is a seventeen-year veteran of professional sport and a former team captain, who experienced numerous coaching styles over his long career. Cliff said, "It's important to know your players, to understand their differences and work with them accordingly. For example, introverts and extroverts are different. Some players need to calm down. Others need to pump up. As a coach, I would try to communicate with players in a way that would help them understand and learn what they need to do to be better." Darby Hendrickson, another fifteen-year veteran and former captain, agrees: "You can't treat everyone the same. Players and circumstances are different. I think coaching is most effective when it has an awareness of those differences and a feel for what's needed in the moment."[16]

Of course a leader can't always be responsive to the players' diverse needs, nor can he or she accordingly provide different messages and feedback for each individual. However, as a leader it is important to have an ear to the heart of the team and to know who you are, whom you are coaching, and what is likely to help the team move in the desired direction. Similarly, as a team member, one must flex and adapt to leadership styles that may not be a perfect match—and when appropriate, communicate to leadership what works best. Coaching is an up and down process. Frequently, leadership's ear and voice are strengthened and improved with a solid coach-core leadership relationship.

Leadership is undoubtedly a key to team success. The mind leads and the body follows. And leadership is both a vertical and horizontal phenomenon. It's about having vision, about knowing what it takes to win, and how and when to communicate that message. Then it's about walking your talk and enrolling your people.

EVALUATE:

Evaluate your team's leadership.

On a scale of 1–10 rate team leadership from the top down.

1 2 3 4 5 6 7 8 9 10

poor   excellent

Do you feel the vertical or top down leaders in your organization fulfill the requirements of their positions? If not, is there anything that can be done about this? If so, what?

On a scale of 1–10 rate core leadership from the rank and file.

1 2 3 4 5 6 7 8 9 10

poor   excellent

Do you feel the core leaders in your organization fulfill the requirements of their positions? If not, is there anything that can be done about this? If so, what?

What leadership qualities do you possess?

Do you consider yourself a leader within your team?

Is there an opportunity for you to participate in and/or increase your leadership role in a way that will contribute to team success? If so, how?

CHAPTER 4

THE GAME PLAN

Winning teams have a clear direction.

Only through focus can you create world class results,
no matter how capable you are.
—Bill Gates[1]

Vision without action is fantasy. Action without vision
is random activity.

Hard work is a key to success. However, winning is more than just working hard. It's working smart. It's having a direction and focus. It's having a plan and working the plan. A plan involves defining what has to be done, how to go about doing it, who will do it, and setting time lines. With winning teams it's very much about everyone working the plan *together*. Working the plan is an expression of organization, direction, and cooperation. It involves a coordinated effort by a group of people directing their energy efficiently and effectively along specific lines.

People often refer to luck when they speak of winners and winning. When it comes to luck, I embrace Branch Rickey's comment,

"Luck is the residue of design."[2] Winning teams create both their design and their luck.

When Vince Lombardi, the legendary football coach, was asked by a prominent industrialist, "What makes a winning team?" Lombardi cited several key qualities that make a team a winner. The first thing he said was, "The players have to know their jobs."[3] Even Pellerud agrees. When I talked with Pellerud, a World Cup winning soccer coach regarding his thoughts on team success, he offered two keys. The first is, "a clearly established 'philosophy'—a way to play the game." His second key is "clear individual roles within this philosophy, which the players understand, accept, and respect."[4] Bottom line, the players have to know their jobs.

It's the same in business. In discussing corporate success, Steve Kerr, who held the title chief learning officer for both GE and Goldman Sachs, has said, "First you need to tell people exactly what is expected of them. Not the mumbo jumbo about making the company or the division the best or biggest in the world, but specifically what role Mr. Salesman or Ms. Engineer are supposed to play in this great enterprise." Kerr continues, "Once you know specifically what you want your employees to be doing in the future, then you need to measure it."[5]

Focus is a key to success. Winning teams share a winning focus. There's an awareness of where they're going, what has to be done, and a belief in their capability as a group to execute the plan. It is generally the role of top down leadership to create the mission statement and define the game plan, and the job of core leadership and the rank and file to see that the plan is effectively implemented.

Whether in business, sport, healthcare, or the arts, the most impressive team meetings I have ever witnessed took place when I was working with the Rams of the National Football League. Every Monday morning at 9:00 am the team's thirteen coaches would meet around a conference table at the Rams' training facility to create the plan for the following week. First, they would analyze and discuss the game the team had played the previous (Sunday) afternoon. They would explore what the team did well on offense. Then they would go over what they did well on defense. The question that followed was, "What can we do to insure that we can continue to do these things well?" Suggestions were made and notes were taken. Next, they explored what the team did poorly in yesterday's contest, on offense . . . and then defense. And again, the question was asked: What can we do to improve performance so that we can execute more effectively in these areas?

In his research for the book *Good to Great*, author Jim Collins[6] described a quality of winning organizations as the relative absence of discussion about what he called "competitive strategy." He noted that while these organizations did discuss strategy and winning, they did not define their strategies *principally* in response to what others were doing. Instead, they focused primarily on what *they* were working to create, and how *they* were trying to improve relative to an absolute standard of excellence.

Daniel Lamarre, the president of Cirque du Soleil, also believes that focusing on what the competition is doing can be limiting. Lamarre has said, "If you want to have a breakthrough, don't look around—look ahead."[7]

Back to the Rams story, it was only *after* team performance was assessed that the question was asked, "Who do we face this week?" At this point two coaches who had spent the entire previous week analyzing video of the Rams' next opponent stepped forward with a computer printout detailing the play patterns, strengths, and weaknesses of the Rams' next opponent. That information was reviewed and then two practical questions were explored: What can we do to exploit their weaknesses? And what can we do to neutralize their strengths? In that two-hour, interactive meeting of coaching minds, directions were defined, decisions made, plays selected, and a practical plan of action was formulated. In the five days that followed, the players were trained to implement the plan. Then, on the following Sunday, it was "show time" and the team and the plan was tested. A day after that, the Monday morning meeting was repeated.

This week-long exercise was one of the most striking demonstrations I've observed of a group of specialists working together, defining a plan, communicating it to the team, training them in its execution, and then seeing the team implement the plan under pressure. And then reviewing the team's success with the same exercise the following week. It was the kind of organization and direction in action that is key to winning team performance.

Discussing the Rams' planning process with Alan Brahmst, a former Olympian, now a strategist in the telecommunications industry, we touched on another interesting parallel between business and sport. After listening to my description of the Rams' planning process, Alan said with some surprise, "Your description of how the Rams create a game plan is fundamentally SWOT analysis."[8] He went on to explain that in SWOT analysis, the S stands for strength. It's what we do well and must continue to do well. The W stands for weakness. It's what we have to improve in our process to be successful. The O stands for opportunity. It's what we can and should exploit in the market. And the T stands for threat, and it's something we have to defend. SWOT is a useful model for developing and maintaining effective team performance.

Football, more than any sport, is the game of the plan. The plan is formulated by a select group of leaders (the coaching staff), who pass it down (vertically) to the players. The players' task is to implement the plan. While some sports like basketball, hockey, and soccer are more horizontal and more "flow games" (see Chapter 11), to be successful the participants on any team must understand team directives or strategy and be organized and able to execute. Indeed, what Lombardi and Kerr have said applies to all team situations: "The players have to know their job."

Shortly after working with the Rams, I ran an interdisciplinary clinic treating pain and disability. One of our major clients was a large insurance company who referred their clients to us for rehabilitation. I recall enthusiastically discussing our positive results with the vice president of the insurance group and suggesting that he implement a plan of action that would afford more of his company's claimants the opportunity to experience the benefits of our rehab program. The vice president, who was relatively new at his job and was proceeding cautiously, replied that it would probably be another six months before he would get around to reviewing procedures and could consider making any changes.

"Six months," I exclaimed, "why, when I worked with the Rams we would create a plan in a matter of hours, act on it immediately, and assess it a few days later."

Somewhat miffed, the vice president replied, "Well, I'm running an insurance company, not a football team."

Pro sport provides an exemplary model in regard to many aspects of effective team performance. Because it is so intensely competitive, a clear plan of action is vital to success, and that plan must be continually assessed, refined, and adjusted as new weekly challenges present themselves. In the high-profile, high-pressure world of pro sport waiting months or even weeks to make functional management decisions simply isn't good enough.

To what extent is the decline of the major car manufacturers in North America due to not having an adaptive game plan or strategy? General Motors' drop in market share can be attributed in part to leadership's apparent inability to predict and adapt, keys to a winning game plan.

Instead of building fuel efficient models like the hybrids, GM adopted a bigger is better strategy. In addition, GM committed to costly labor agreements (made decades ago) which failed to predict increased life expectancy and rising health care costs. As one GM business manager related, "The near-sightedness of senior management has burdened us with significant legacy costs (health and pension benefits) that add thousands to the cost of producing a vehicle."

In contrast, Toyota, now the world's number one auto company, deserves kudos for their strategy and systems. Toyota is renowned for their long-term planning and their ability to adapt and innovate. They are leaders in hybrid technology. They can get new models from the drawing board to production more quickly than the competition. And, their lean, efficient, production system (TPS) is modeled by industries all over the planet.[9]

In his book *The Toyota Way*, Jeffery K. Liker summarizes TPS process and strategy with the following seven factors: "create process 'flow' to surface problems, use pull systems to avoid overproduction, level out the workload, stop when there is a quality problem, standardize tasks for continuous improvement, use visual control so no problems are hidden, and use only reliable, thoroughly tested technology."[10] (The Toyota example is discussed more fully in Chapter 10.)

One championship hockey team I worked with also defined seven success factors that contributed to their team's success. Players were told, "If we perform to these success factors we will be successful." Their success factors included very specific performance measures (for example, 70 hits or blocked shots per game, 80 percent zone clears, fewer than three odd man rushes against). The players not only knew exactly what these success factors were, they were also coached to understand exactly how these factors contributed to team success. After each game, players were given specific feedback from the coaching staff as to how effectively they were implementing these success factors, which were key elements of their game plan. A team with a clear plan of action, that knows what to do, why they are doing it, and how to do it, will be likely to succeed.

Under pressure, leaders often exhort their charges to "work harder," "be more aggressive," or "raise the bar." I encourage leadership to be specific. It's important that their people understand what is meant by these charged urgings. Specific success factors supply that clarity. If the team members don't understand the specifics of what is meant by raising the bar, the pressure engendered by simply demanding "more" can produce stress and anxiety, and less than the desired results.

Creating Your Personal Action Plan

Many of my clients are under considerable pressure to perform and succeed. Pressure, and the anxiety it engenders, often causes contraction, producing a narrowing, limiting, negative perspective.

One antidote to tension-induced contraction is to create and mentally rehearse a goal-directed plan of action. The process begins by creating ease instead of dis-ease. To create a relaxed state, a process I go through with my clients involves having them sit comfortably and then bring their attention to their breathing. Paying attention to one's breathing is a simple and powerful way to integrate mind and body.

- I encourage clients to slip into the rhythm of the breath.

By that I mean to experience/feel the breath flowing in then, to experience/feel the breath flowing out.

Relaxed, rhythmical breathing improves the quality and clarity of thought and expands one's conception of positive possibility. (Too frequently under pressure people focus on the negative, on what could go wrong.)

- After a few minutes of relaxed rhythmical breathing, I ask them what they are working towards. I ask them to complete the statement, "When I am performing at my best I _____."

- I want them to be clear enough in defining what their optimal performance is like that they can actually visualize doing it.

- Next, to expand context I direct them to visualize themselves integrating their performance into their team's performance.

Creating a plan of action should evolve out of an ideal image, a success image, not from an image charged with anxiety or a fear of failure.

- I then encourage them to work back to the source of their success. I might say, "After you explore the success image in your mind and experience *what performing well looks and feels* like . . . ask yourself what will it take in resources, organization, and preparation for me to create that performance."

Consider the challenges and obstacles you may encounter. Imagine successfully overcoming any or all of them.

Create a preparation routine or "pre-game plan" to help you to perform consistently well. Routine strengthens consistency. The plan need not be rigid and fixed; it can be fluid and flexible. And it should be consistent with the overall team plan. See the "coach" if there is any uncertainty regarding role or process.

Merlin Olsen, an NFL All Pro and Hall of Fame player with the Los Angeles Rams, underlined the importance of having a clear plan. "We need to know where we are going and how we plan to get there. Our dreams and aspirations must be translated into tangible goals, with priorities and a time frame. All this should be in writing so it can be reviewed, updated, and revised as necessary."[11]

The pattern of defining what has to be done, communicating it to team members, rehearsing, executing the plan, and then assessing and adjusting is key to success in most endeavors. As the coach said, "The players have to know their jobs."

Focus is key to superior performance, and the plan is a blueprint for focus.

The ABCs to Success

A part of my work enhancing individual and team performance is assisting clients to define and establish a clear, personal performance pattern. It's what I call their ABCs. These ABCs break down their role (whatever the job) into three basic functional tasks. Their ABCs should be clear enough that they can actually visualize them.

For Brooks, a pro pitcher, his ABCs were very technical:

A. stay on top (arm angle),
B. keep the ball down (location), and
C. follow through (motion).

The ABCs of Martin, a sales representative for Fieldturf, a leading sport surface company, were these:

A. know the product (its features),
B. know the customer (their needs and interests), and
C. determine who is the decision maker I have to address.

To reiterate, in preparing to perform I usually suggest that clients take a couple of minutes to relax, breathe, and see themselves (visualize) performing their ABCs . . . and performing well and integrating that into the team process. Defining and then rehearsing their ABCs can keep people on track and support effective performance, even under pressure.

One of my favorite sayings is "Vision without action is fantasy. And action without vision is random activity." Know your job. Think positive. Think ABC. You get more of what you think about. See yourself performing well. Then do it.

EVALUATE:

What is your primary goal(s)?

Does your team have a clear game plan that is going to help it achieve its goal?

Can you articulate that plan?

On a scale of 1–10 rate your confidence in your team's game plan or strategy.

1 2 3 4 5 6 7 8 9 10
poor   excellent

Is the strategy clearly understood? Is it credible?

Do you have/know your specific role in that game plan? (If not, how can you get clarity about this?)

What do you need to do and achieve to insure your part of the plan is realized?

Assuming you know your personal game plan, what are your ABCs that will insure you do your job appropriately?

List any suggestions to improve the overall understanding, communication, and implementation of team strategy.

CHAPTER 5

COMMITMENT

Winning teams pay the price.

Failure is not an option.
—Gene Kranz, Apollo 13 Mission Control Flight Director[1]

You've got to use the immense energy that exists in the company,
the immense desire to please, to win, to achieve . . . this is how we do it,
by hook or crook we'll get it done . . . there's not an I can't do it factor,
there's always a way to do it.
—Jackie Stewart, Team Principal, Jaguar Racing[2]

To be a winner one must be totally committed . . . Total commitment means
being willing to do whatever is necessary to become successful. One must be
willing to work hard, to push themselves physically until it hurts . . . To be a
winner one must be willing to make sacrifices . . . If you want to be a winner
you will give up anything that does not help you become better at your sport.
All athletes are not endowed with the same physical abilities. One can and
many before you have overcome a lack of ability with extra effort.
These people are totally committed.
—Forest Gregg, NFL Hall of Fame player and coach[3]

Commitment is a major key to team success. In team terms, commitment means two things. First, it's a willingness to do whatever it takes in creativity, effort, determination, discipline, and perseverance to achieve the team's goal. Second, commitment is a surrendering of ego of the individual "I" for the group "we."

Commitment = The Willingness to Do What's Necessary

While many people set goals, far fewer are willing to do what it takes to realize their goals. Commitment means paying the price. Winning team members believe their goal is relevant, possible, and worthy of the effort and sacrifice. They are willing to follow leadership's direction and exercise the necessary focus, effort, and discipline to prepare. The result is a group of individuals determined to do whatever they can to achieve their goal . . . and willing to work hard and long to make it happen.

There is a gravitational effect to team commitment. By that I mean commitment usually flows from the top down. One example was Chinese leadership making the decision for China to become a dominant player on the world's competitive sport scene. The decision, made at the highest level, was to showcase Chinese capability by winning as many medals as possible at the 2008 Olympics, which China was hosting. China committed the money, resources, and people-power to achieve excellence in a variety of sports, including some (like trampoline) that were previously foreign to the Chinese.

When trampoline was first designated as an Olympic sport, the Chinese sent twenty coaches to the world championships to observe. They then imported a team of international coaches to train their coaches and athletes. A dozen years later their men and women athletes were world champions, and gold medalists at the 2008 Olympic

Games. Between 1988 and 2008, China increased their total Olympic medal production 400 percent and their gold medal acquisition an astonishing 1000 percent. The achievement was a product of a commitment that filtered top down into programs where athletes were selected early, trained by skilled coaches for eight hours a day, six days a week, eleven months a year . . . for years.

Top-down commitment is also a part of corporate transformation. As we sat together on a flight across the country, Mark D, a corporate change specialist who consults with the banking industry, explained, the process of effectively facilitating corporate change. According to him, "It inevitably begins with a sponsor, a senior leader in the organization who commits to the change. Then the players (project managers, change facilitators, etc.) are brought in to implement the process." He continued, "Of course, it is important to collaborate with and enroll the rank and file, but the commitment to evolve flows top down."

On a smaller scale, David Wolfe, a young entrepreneur growing a successful specialty clothing company, is a model of commitment. He has a significant financial obligation to the bank, a sizable home mortgage, and a family with two small children to support. He described feeling pressure every day. When I asked him his take on why teams win he said, "In my world, failure is not an option." That phrase, "failure is not an option," was a rallying cry issued by Gene Kranz, the lead flight director for Mission Control, to the ground crew team in Houston in their efforts to bring the wounded Apollo 13 spacecraft and their crew safely back to earth.[4] The term implies total commitment.

When I asked David how the phrase translated into an operating philosophy for his manufacturing team, he replied, "In our business we deliver quality products to specific events. If I tell a customer that an order will be delivered on time, quality product will be delivered on time. We won't fail. Each order is important to the person who ordered it. They want to look good. I am passionate that we honor our commitment. 'Failure is not an option' is an all-encompassing philosophy within our company. Bottom line is, we deliver. We never fail. That is our commitment."

David went on to explain how he managed to meet this commitment. "I just work twice as hard as anybody else. I continually ask myself, and my team, how can we do things better? What are the barriers that limit us? And how can we overcome them? If we need more training in a specific area, we train harder and better. If we're not focusing, we find a way to improve our focus. If there's something holding me back, like my temper, then we put people in place who are more patient than I am, who understand the needs or the customer and can empathize with them better then I can. It's our dedication to being the best we can be . . . and it works for us. Like Nike, we just do it."[5]

A graphic description of commitment was Wayne Gretzky's observation of the New York Islanders immediately after they defeated his Edmonton Oilers to win the Stanley Cup. "We were all defeated and down. We walked by the Islanders' dressing room. They were celebrating and their guys had ice packs on their shoulders, their jaws, and their knees. A lot of them would have to have operations. We realized then what they had done to win. We said to each other, 'Hey, now we know what it takes. You gotta put your face in front of slap shots, take a punch in the face, you gotta sacrifice—that's what winning is.'"[6] No more lessons were necessary. After that demonstration of commitment, Gretzky and the Edmonton Oilers went on to win a remarkable five Stanley Cups in the next seven years.

I frequently speak to management and coaching groups on personal excellence, teamwork, and leadership. In the past two years while writing the book I have asked several thousand people from a diversity of groups (corporate executives, managers, and sales teams in a variety of industries, as well as coaches, and professional and Olympic sport teams) this question: "Please rank the following five qualities in terms of their relative contribution to team success. The five qualities are talent, leadership, strategy, commitment, and chemistry." I acknowledge that each quality is vital to success and that these qualities all interact with each other. Yet *every* group asked rated commitment as the most important of the five team qualities presented.

Question: Does commitment follow success? Or does success follow commitment? The answer is something of both. Clearly, success follows commitment. Teams that are enrolled and willing to pay the price achieve results. However, individually and collectively, there must be a perceived payoff for the effort. Some success is necessary along the way to nurture and sustain the commitment. People are reluctant to keep knocking themselves out if they feel their efforts are fruitless.

After a very successful season that culminated in a disappointing loss in the NFC championship game (the winner goes to the Super Bowl) I watched our players return to training camp the following season with added drive and determination. They understood how close they had come to winning it all. They knew the team possessed the talent and know-how to be successful and with just a little more commitment they could make it happen. That commitment was evident in the focus and effort expended in practice and in the weight room, as well as the way they spoke to each other, and the effort they consistently put out on the field. Success nurtures commitment and commitment is part of the character of winning teams.

On numerous occasions I've listened to coaches prod a team to raise their level of performance and give a little more. A favorite motivational urging is to explain to the players the significance of just one more degree of temperature. The spiel goes as follows. At 211 degrees Fahrenheit water won't boil but with just a rise of one degree in temperature, water begins to boil producing steam. Steam is power. It possesses the power to drive giant turbines and to move mountains. In this classic motivational pitch, the coach goes on to describe how "with just one degree more of commitment and effort from each of you, we can generate the power to achieve a remarkable result." I've observed coaches use this example in an attempt to lift team performance in North America and Europe. The story (and sometimes the response) is the same; the only difference is that outside the USA the one degree is from 99 to 100 centigrade.

Commitment = The *We* Is Greater Than the *Me*

Vince Lombardi's second response to the question "Why do teams win?" was, "In winning teams the we is greater than the me."[7] By that he meant on winning teams each team member is willing to surrender and sacrifice his or her ego and personal agenda to serve the team. Many veteran pro athletes and leaders have underlined the importance of a collective attitude for team success that "nothing is bigger than the team." Sayings like "It is amazing how much you can accomplish when it doesn't matter who gets the credit"; "The star of the team is the team"; "There is no *I* in "team"; and "Teamwork, simply stated, is less me and more we" may be trite, but they highlight something that is very real. People committed, enrolled, surrendering ego, and willing to work together can achieve incredible results.

Lou Holz, a legendary team builder, defined lack of commitment as a cause for team failure. Holz said, "I inherited five losing football teams in my coaching career. If you asked me if these squads had anything in common, I would say yes. They were all largely composed of athletes who moaned about everything. You cannot turn around teams like that unless you rehabilitate the malcontents or sweep them from their rosters . . . Superior players don't complain about restrictions, they take pride in them. They understand their willingness to sacrifice places them among that rare breed of individuals who are willing to do whatever is necessary to attain their goals . . . . People with average skills often attain greatness because they are willing to pay a price for it. You may not be able to outthink, out-market or outspend your competition, but you can outwork them."[8]

Accompanying "buy in" is the belief that making the commitment—that is, putting in the time, the effort, and the energy—will lead to the desired result. Winners believe in what their team is about (regarding both their team's mission and manner of implementation) and they are willing to sacrifice and do whatever is asked of them to achieve the team's goals.

Goldman Sachs, a 100 billion dollar organization with 20,000 employees worldwide is a leader in their industry. When I asked a successful veteran player with GS what made the firm so successful he said, "It's the culture and the commitment. It's all about teamwork" He continued, "At Goldman Sachs people are incentivized for building consensus and working together, and we're penalized for saying the word "I" or what's in it for me?" We have a lot of big egos and high paid personalities but we all work together . . . . And we work for the firm." This kind of team think is a learned behavior. In her book, *Goldman Sachs, The Culture of Success*, Lisa Endlich explains how GS uses a combination of careful personnel selection (upwards of twenty interviews are carried out looking for players with suitable intellect and team orientation), along with strong leadership, management coaching, clear guidelines, and a payout system that rewards successful team play to shape a *team mindset* in an industry which is decidedly "me oriented."[9]

Glen was a highly successful, professional athlete, who competed well in the professional game for over 15 seasons. He presented himself as a reliable team player dedicated to being the best he could be and consistently doing what was best for the team. I consulted with him for most of his professional career and repeatedly observed him adjust to different coaching changes and challenges, including some that dramatically altered his role with the team. What was most significant was his response to leadership. When he believed in the direction presented by the head coach (which was 95 percent of the time), he willingly did what was asked to the best of his ability. When he didn't believe (sometimes because he thought the decisions were arbitrary or not carefully thought out), he struggled mightily with expressing his commitment. The point is that commitment is not only a function of the character of the player, it also correlates with the individual's belief and trust in leadership.

Earlier I mentioned the incident at Chicago airport when I ran into a veteran coach who had been the head coach of several successful National Hockey League teams. While we waited for our flights, I asked him his opinion as to why teams win. The coach, who had a reputation as being very thorough and "systems-oriented," said, "Look back at the teams that have been successful in winning the Stanley Cup over the past decade." He listed half a dozen. "They all used different systems," he said. "Clearly it's not the system per se that's important. Rather, it's the players' willingness to buy into the system, and their ability to execute it that leads to success."[10]

A challenge for leadership on any kind of team is to get team members to buy in. As business and sport teams become more diverse in composition, this becomes more and more of a challenge. For example, the talent on many professional sport teams in baseball, basketball, hockey, and soccer is increasingly an international mix from the Americas, Europe, and Asia. These men grew up in different cultures, speak different languages, play a variety of different styles, and are paid inordinate sums of money—often more than the coach—to perform. It's a challenge to blend these elements into a cohesive competitive unit. To do so, the coach must communicate a vision, "this is a way we can win," and get the players to trust and commit to executing the system. With team success, players are reinforced for giving their all. However, the players' commitment is necessary to win in the first place.

I asked Vic Rapp, a veteran NFL and CFL coach I worked with in both football leagues, what it took to win. I'll always remember his response. He said, "Saul, there are three ingredients to team success. First, you've got to have the talent. Second, you've got to have the game plan." Then, he paused, smiled, and said, "Third, and this one is the toughest, you've got to get the talent to perform the game plan."[11]

I met with the manager of a major league baseball team that was losing more frequently than it was winning. We sat in the clubhouse before the game discussing several factors that contribute to team success, including leadership. The manager, a very team-minded individual, related that one of the challenges he was facing was presented by the team's star player. "He has a ton of talent but he is not a team guy." The star didn't conform to team rules. What particularly upset the manager was that this player was consistently late for meetings. The manager explained how he posted the time for team meetings on a board in the clubhouse each day. However, the star player was so consistently late that eventually the manager stopped posting the time to avoid highlighting the star's nonconformance to team policy. What further upset the manager was that the star, though making over ten million dollars a year, refused to pay the fines the team set for being late.

This high-profile player's egocentricity, instead of modeling positive team behavior, was setting a negative example and compromising the leader's ability to manage. The manager said, "I know players are thinking, 'What's going on? Are there two sets of rules here? One for him and one for the rest of us?'" The impact on team morale was apparent and untenable. The question was, what to do about it?

The "star player" example highlights something I've observed over the years. Organizations and teams are much more inclined to bend their rules to accommodate their stars than the rank and file.

Compromise can be unhealthy, even dangerous, when the star's behavior is egocentric and doesn't reflect a commitment to the organization or team goals. It is also an example of the inter-relatedness of the players (a team is a group of animals hitched together . . . if one of the dogs pulls off course all the other dogs are affected), as well as the inter-connectedness of the nine keys. In any organization, commitment affects identity, which affects chemistry, which affects leadership, which in turn affects commitment. Contrast this star player's behavior with the perspective presented earlier by Steve Yzerman's comment, "I always try and do what's best for the team," and it's not difficult to understand why the baseball star just mentioned has consistently played on losing teams while Yzerman won every major championship he pursued.

The marriage of talent, leadership, and commitment is key to winning teams in any field. Ellen was the manager in a corporation that encouraged its players to exercise initiative and grow their entrepreneurial spirit. When Ellen, a bright, aspiring, entrepreneurial type exercised initiative on a project, her boss felt she was overstepping her bounds, reprimanded her, and moved her a notch back in the corporate hierarchy. The boss felt Ellen was someone he couldn't control and that she was a threat to his management. On the other hand, Ellen felt that her boss's response was unfair and personal and didn't reflect the corporate identity. "What I did may have been unorthodox but it was in the best interest of the organization," explained Ellen. "He is more concerned with himself and keeping everyone under his control than acting in a way that best serves this organization."

I was unable to determine who was "right." Indeed, it seemed there was a kernel of truth to what both parties were saying. My challenge was to create understanding, respect, and harmony between manager and boss. What is clear, however (at any level of an organization), is that when a team member's "me" is bigger than the collective "we," the team usually knows it, and the team suffers. Harmony supports commitment: egocentricity, suspicion, and disharmony destroy it.

Often leadership has to shape team commitment. Shaping is a process of building behavior by rewarding gradual approximations of the desired end behavior. When I took over the leadership of an interdisciplinary clinic, the staff was skeptical that they would ever receive a bonus. The previous owners had promised them performance bonuses for several years but, when calculations were made at the end of the fiscal year, it always seemed that they fell a little short. After taking control I communicated clear performance targets for the team. At the end of our first year, although the team had significantly increased performance, they just missed hitting the target we had set. However, because it was our first year and I wanted to acknowledge their positive effort, they were given a bonus anyway. The bonus was a statement underlining the fact that a new style of leadership was at play and indicating that new management would acknowledge their commitment and their success. They responded with record performances in the following four years.

I discussed winning with Jon, a successful bank manager whose team had been chosen the top branch in the organization for a couple of years running. He said, "Two key ingredients that go into creating a winning team are talent and strategy. But talent and strategy aren't always enough." (As Coach Rapp said earlier, the toughest challenge for a coach is to get the talent to execute the plan effectively). In addition to talent and strategy, the bank manager highlighted *trust*, specifically trust in leadership. He explained, "People must know what the leader stands for. They must believe in you and in your expertise. And they must trust that you are committed to doing what is in the best interest of the organization. Sure, talent is a key factor. However, trust in leadership moves talent to commit and perform."

Jackie Stewart has experienced every aspect of the Formula 1 racing business. He has been a World Champion driver, a team owner, and a board advisor to the sport. Jackie believes success in Formula 1 is teamwork-related, and that trusting the leader and trusting one another is the glue that integrates a winning team. It extends top down, bottom up, and throughout the organization. Stewart has said, "Team leaders should never compromise their integrity. Being able to respect the people you are working with, to depend on them, to trust them is extremely important . . . . It's trust . . . you can't buy it."[12]

When I reviewed the nine qualities that characterize winning teams with management guru and author Henry Mintzberg,[13] the quality he chose to comment on was commitment. Henry underlined the importance of commitment in successful organizations, both among the players (the rank and file), and senior leadership's commitment to the organization. "And," he added, "unfortunately, these days the commitment of leadership to their organization is frequently and dramatically lacking in the corporate sector." Reports of vanishing trust, and corporate leadership profiting the "me" rather than the "we," appear to be epidemic.

Senior leadership in sport appears to be more focused on the "we" and the team than are many business leaders. That said, whether it's sport, business, or government, commitment to the team and respect for team members is a core quality of team success. And trust in the competency and values of leadership promotes team commitment.

There are a few exceptions in which collective "buy in" may be less vital to team success. One is on sales teams, where members are frequently independent operators supervised by a manager but essentially driven by individual financial incentives based on their personal performance. Baseball is similar in that players are often paid incentives based more on their personal statistics than on team performance.

After taking over the leadership of an investment services team, "DL" asked what he could do to build more of a team sense within the group. I acknowledged that in these situations where the "I," more than the "we," is the driving force, it's challenging to enroll team members in the overall success of the group. However, in money-game situations, unless there is some incentive payoff for team success, such as giving team members a small percentage of the overall group's success, the tendency will remain for players to focus on their own performance numbers with relatively little commitment to the overall team's effort.

One insurance sales team I worked with increased their sales volume over 100 percent in the six months we worked together. Two of the reasons for the rise in performance were the talent of the group and the commitment of Michael Campany, their sales manager, who was willing to do whatever was necessary to support and enroll team members in the success of the group. Michael believed his team could be top performers. To that end, he personally reviewed tapes, CDs, journals, and books, and attended professional development seminars (including one of my own on personal excellence) to discover any suitable training aid that he could utilize to motivate and support team members. He even funded these explorations himself. Michael's shared sense of what was possible for the team and his commitment to making that possibility a reality contributed to some outstanding results.

What I did working with his group was to get them to take responsibility for their thinking and their actions. In group sessions we practiced psycho-physical exercises to generate (and actually experience) feeling powerful, then I coached team members to envision the success they wanted to achieve, to anticipate and manage any obstacles encountered, and then to commit to actually doing what was necessary to realize their goals. I encouraged them to acknowledge themselves and each other and to use any challenge to refocus on the positive.

When discussing commitment with managers, coaches and elite performers, two qualities frequently find their way into the conversation: perseverance and discipline. I see both of these performance behaviors as basic expressions of commitment.

1. Perseverance Is the Quality of a Winner

Nothing in this world can take the place of persistence. Talent will not; nothing is more common than unsuccessful men with talent. Genius will not; unrewarded genius is almost a proverb. Education will not; the world is full of educated derelicts. Persistence and determination are omnipotent. The slogan 'press on' has solved and always will solve the problems of the human race.

—Calvin Coolidge[14]

There are many great examples in sport of athletes who were told they did not have the right stuff, or individuals who overcame serious illness and injury, and, despite the odds, persisted and ultimately achieved at the highest level.

I learned the benefits of perseverance early in my career. Shortly after I began working as a sport psychologist I was fortunate to have contributed to some impressive results at the collegiate level. One of my collegiate baseball clients experienced a 300 percent performance increment and tied the NCAA record for most home runs in a single season. At the same time I consulted with the university's golf team, which went, in the coach's opinion, "from being losers into winners."

The techniques I used then (and still use today) apply to individuals as well as teams and involve managing focus, emotions, and attitude. The collegiate athletes responded very well. I began working with professional teams, first in baseball, then football. But despite early successes it was a challenge to sell the resource and create an opportunity to consult at the highest professional levels.

I recall telephoning the head coach of one NHL team and leaving several messages with his secretary. When he didn't return my call I called again, again, again, and again. I must have called and left seven or eight messages, but still there was no return call. Finally, on my eighth or ninth call, he picked up the phone. When I said, "It's Dr. Saul Miller speaking," his response was a somewhat sarcastic, "Well, you certainly are persistent."

I replied, "Persistence is the quality of a winner. You expect your players to persist in the game. Don't you?"

His mood shifted. He laughed and said, "Yes, I do." I said that I wanted an opportunity to meet with him to explain what I could do to help his team be more successful. Somewhat unenthusiastically he agreed to an appointment. We met in his office several days later. Shortly thereafter he referred several players to me. When I began to work with the team it was midseason and they had won only two of their previous twenty-one games. The team's performance picked up, they made it into the playoffs, kept winning, and went all the way to the Stanley Cup finals.

My comment, "Persistence is the quality of a winner," appeared to open a door to our meeting. It changed his thinking, from "This guy is a nuisance" to "This person is determined." My perseverance came from a sincere belief that I had something useful to contribute.

Winning players and winning teams are positive. They believe in themselves. They believe in the goal they are working towards and in the process that will get them there. Whether it's pitching a concept or a baseball, that belief stimulates them to act and persevere.

2. Discipline Is Another Characteristic of Commitment and Winning

The word comes from the Latin word disciplina, which relates to "instructions given to a disciple," and the "order necessary for instruction." As such, discipline can be seen as the order necessary to express commitment and achieve success.

Basketball legendary coach Bob Knight sees discipline and commitment as one. "It has always been my thought that the most important single ingredient in success in athletics or life is discipline. I have many times felt that this word is the most ill-defined in our language. My definition of the word is: Do what has to be done. When it has to be done. As well as it can be done. And do it that way all the time."[15]

Lateral inhibition is a neurological concept that describes a remarkable focusing mechanism we all possess. It lets us determine the precise locus of a stimulus. For instance, when skin is touched, the sensory neurons in the skin, at the point being stimulated, "fire." To help us to determine the exact location of the stimulus, the neurons stimulated also suppress the firing of neighboring neurons. The amount of inhibition is proportional to the amount of stimulation. The more powerful the stimulus, the more powerful the inhibition to adjacent cells.

Winning is about a sustained focus. To achieve success the members of a team have to maintain a focus on what is relevant, and tune out all those stimuli (however appealing and alluring) that could be seen as distracting or irrelevant. To succeed they have to maintain "the order necessary for instruction" and execution. That is, they have to execute discipline.

Vince Lombardi,[16] a renowned disciplinarian, once labeled Green Bay Packer superstar and Hall of Famer Forrest Gregg "the finest player I ever coached." Not surprisingly, Gregg linked discipline to commitment and extolled the importance of discipline in individual and team success. "I believe in discipline. You can forgive incompetence. You can forgive lack of ability. But one thing you can't ever forgive is a lack of discipline."[17]

We have said commitment is the willingness to do what's necessary to get the job done. Roger Neilson, an innovative and dedicated coach, once said, "Winning is not about playing one great game. It's about playing well night, after night, after night."[18] That means learning how to maintain the necessary focus, discipline, and balance to consistently give your best. If a team member is not self-disciplining, then the team must create a disciplining structure. And winning teams do that.

Commitment is key to winning. Commitment is expressed in working smart, long and hard, and working well. Commitment is about determination, persistence, and discipline. Commitment is a function of belief and trust; in leadership, the plan, each other, and one's self. On that last point, some interesting research on leadership shows that teams are most effective when people feel good about both the leader . . . and themselves.

EVALUATE:

In Chapter 5 we observed that commitment is expressed in determination, perseverance, and discipline. On a scale of 1–10, rate your present level of commitment in each of these areas.

Rate your present level of determination.

> 1 2 3 4 5 6 7 8 9 10
> poor   excellent

Rate your present level of perseverance.

> 1 2 3 4 5 6 7 8 9 10
> poor   excellent

Rate your present level of discipline.

> 1 2 3 4 5 6 7 8 9 10
> poor   excellent

In each of these areas, what needs to change for you to increase your level of commitment?

What about the rest of your team? What would you say is the average level of commitment of the group?

List any suggestions to increase team enrollment or team commitment.

CHAPTER 6

FEEDBACK

Winning teams know the score.

Effective feedback is a key to team success. It consists of two basic elements:

- The score. Winning teams need an objective, accurate way to measure their performance.

- Acknowledgement. The players in successful organizations benefit from acknowledgement and criticism of how they are doing.

The Score

If you play to win, then you gotta keep score.

To be successful a team needs to know how they are doing. They need high-quality, objective feedback. *They need to know the score.* The ability to assess and adjust performance is critical to continuous improvement. Assessment must be based on clear and accurate information. Team members may think, "We're a great team." "We're winners." And, "We're doing fine." However, if the results of their actions don't translate into meaningful numbers on some scoreboard, then they may be deluding themselves.

One of the parallels between business and sport is an awareness of and respect for the bottom line. Winning teams know what they have to do to win. They also know that the status quo is never good enough. What won last season rarely repeats. There is a continuous push to be better. The scoreboard is an indicator of how they are doing.

To improve their competitiveness, one professional football team was very aggressive in the off-season, making trades and acquiring some high-priced talent from the free agent market. They spent freely and naturally expected their acquisitions to translate into success. However, five weeks into the season they were winless. Furthermore, they lost three of the first five games decisively. While their performance stimulated analysis and explanation, the scoreboard clearly indicated something was missing.

Similarly, we've all watched manufacturers of everything from Edsel automobiles to soft drinks come out with designer products and new marketing campaigns to challenge existing market classics. The research and marketing behind these new products may have seemed reasonable in corporate offices, but ultimately, when the scoreboard indicated the public wasn't responding and the product wasn't a win, the product line was discontinued.

How do you measure success? Of course, measurement varies depending on the task. *Validity* is all-important. A measure is considered valid if those factors that truly represent team success are being measured. Profitability measures, gross/net income, earnings/expenses, production numbers, quality and defect scores, plus wins, losses, goals, runs, or points scored can all be valid performance indicators. An important question to ask is, "Do the players understand the significance of what is being measured?"

I mentioned earlier that a championship hockey team I worked with defined seven success factors that contributed to success. Players were told if they executed these success factors they would win the game. Their success factors included seven specific performance measures. The players not only knew exactly what these success factors were; they also (and this is important) understood why these factors contributed to team success.

To further improve performance, players were given post-game feedback by the coaching staff in the form of a simple number evaluation based on their ability to execute according to the team's success factors. On some teams the coaches rate the players; on other teams we've had the players rate themselves. With self-rating, it can be helpful to explore with players why they gave themselves that particular score. Participating in the evaluation process develops an appreciation for the task. Individually and collectively, feedback is vital to performance enhancement.

When I ran an interdisciplinary clinic, most of the clinical staff believed that we were one of the best clinics in the country for the particular type of treatment we provided. We measured our outcome in two ways. One was the success rate of clients we treated. Specifically, we measured improvement in their activity levels, reduction in use of medication, their subjective report, and their return to work. The other way we assessed performance was in terms of the financial success of the clinic. I thought it was important for staff members to be aware of both outcome measures. Initially the staff expressed little interest in the clinic's financial performance. They actually expressed resentment about any financial reporting at staff meetings. This was in spite of the fact that the staff received significant performance bonuses relating to the profitability of the clinic.

Their lack of interest in financials persisted until one day I asked team members, "How would you describe the quality of the program we deliver to our patients?" The clinical staff was unanimous in responding that we provided an excellent treatment program, some of the best care and consideration many of the patients had experienced in their entire lives. "Well," I explained, "if we are not fiscally responsible, and if we do not work to keep the clinic profitable, then we will simply not be able to continue providing these patients with a superior-quality treatment experience." When the staff understood the relation of profitability to the continuance of superior clinical service, they took greater interest in the financial reporting (the financial score) and worked harder to make the clinic profitable.

Valid, reliable, well-defined measures of success are critical input to a developing team. These indicators should be understood and agreed upon in advance, so team members know what they are working toward and can determine how they are doing against those predefined standards. At Toyota, a winning organization, employees at each level of the corporation sign off on their annual targets after discussion and agreement with management. Performance in Toyota plants is assessed by meaningful daily and weekly metrics, consisting of clearly defined performance measures assessing quality, efficiency, delivery, and safety. Embracing the all-too-frequent political game of creating a win after the fact by putting a positive spin on whatever results are generated is deceptive, and simply doesn't play long or well in the competitive worlds of business and sport.

In recent years there has been a healthy shift in the corporate world from learned to learning organizations. In essence that's a shift away from more vertical "learned" organizations (they are rigidly structured; leadership is often hierarchical and based on status and past achievement) to more dynamic and horizontal "learning" organizations (where there is a greater willingness to flex and adjust and do whatever it takes to succeed). The shift highlights performance rather than seniority or title as a guiding principle. As such it places a great reliance on quality feedback to determine effective progress.

Microsoft is an example of a successful, learning organization. As David Thielen describes in *The 12 Simple Secrets of Microsoft Management*,[1] the team mantra at Microsoft is "perform, perform, perform." Thielen says, "In a highly competitive success-oriented environment such as Microsoft, you want to succeed because success is the way everyone is measured."[1]

Microsoft measures success at every level of the organization. They use what they call "commitments" to maintain their focus on performance and results. Dan, a fifteen-year Microsoft veteran, explained:

"We call them commitments rather than goals because we're holding ourselves to a higher level of accountability. In effect, we're saying that these are the results we're committed to achieving, rather than just goals that we're directing ourselves toward."

Dan went on to say that Microsoft uses a commitment focus at every layer of the organization, from the highest level, e.g., company-wide business objectives, and goals for individual divisions and product units, all the way down to the work of every individual employee. They use them to: ensure that they meet business objectives, align efforts across organizations, drive priorities at each level of the business, set clear expectations for both managers and employees, and facilitate employee performance reviews.

Microsoft uses both organizational and personal commitments. Dan explained that organizational commitments generally reflect an annual summary of the priorities for an organization within the company. They include multiyear efforts, as well as yearly focus areas or tasks to be completed within one year. Each division or business unit sets performance measures it targets for itself (or has them set by higher-level executives). He said, "Many of our commitments are specific to a given project or software development cycle because that process is so central to what we do as a company. We always have goals associated with an overall product release that provide guiding principles and help motivate the team. We will also have checkpoint goals for individual product milestones, which are shorter periods of product development time. We break our development cycles up into separate milestones, each of which will have their own associated criteria that tell us when we're ready to enter that milestone, and when we're ready to exit. Milestones help us to break long product cycles into manageable chunks, and provide checkpoints to assess our progress."

In addition to organizational targets, Dan explained that all full-time employees at Microsoft work with their managers every year to set personal commitments. Those commitments should be "SMART" (Specific, Measurable, Achievable, Results-based, and Time-specific) so that the employee can be measured against them. Personal commitments should align to the organization's commitments. They will also be influenced by several other factors like: discipline/job title, role in the organization (individual contributor, lead, manager, etc.), career stage/level, specific job responsibilities, and the employee's own interests and career ambitions.

He continued, "At Microsoft, *how you spend your time isn't nearly as important as what you accomplished*, especially in comparison to what you set out to accomplish. Personal commitments force employees to be clear on what they're going to accomplish, and establish clear criteria to assess whether they've achieved or exceeded their goals. Commitments, at their best, are quite crisp (precise). In addition to identifying what you're going to do, you also need to say how you'll do it and what success looks like. In effect, you provide the metrics by which you'll be judged."[2]

I have said repeatedly, the success of the team is the success of its players working together effectively. Dawn, a motivated senior executive, hired a corporate coach to improve her leadership skills. Together they organized a 360-degree survey to assess Dawn's performance. The feedback group consisted of the CEO, Dawn's executive peers, and her direct report subordinates. Their collective response provided Dawn with specific information highlighting her strengths and areas she needed to work on to improve her effectiveness. After receiving the feedback, Dawn and her coach defined several behavior patterns that Dawn committed to working on to improve her performance as a leader. Dawn then informed the entire feedback group of the specific behaviors she was going to work to change/improve. Then after two months, and again after four months, she asked her feedback group how she was progressing in affecting change in these specific areas. Not surprisingly, with her motivation to improve, the specific feedback of the group, and some well-defined behaviors to work on, the response from all levels was that Dawn was doing very well.

A leader at Goldman Sachs also underlined the value of feedback. He said, "My experience with the organization has led me to believe that communication and feedback are the most important elements of the firms "team" success. We have 360-degree reviews where superiors, subordinates, and peers provide team members with feedback and where internal behavior and a team orientation are viewed as performance criteria as important as commercial success."

In any organization, meaningful feedback is vital. The scoreboard is the measuring stick. And assess *and adjust* is the credo for developing and sustaining success.

Accountability and Responsibility

Accountability and responsibility are two qualities often associated with success. When I talk to groups about winning, I often begin with an explanation of how the mind works. I explain that each of us is *response-able* to manage our mind—that is, to create the thoughts and feelings that will generate our success. A first step to becoming more successful in any field is understanding and acknowledging the responsibility each of us has, for how we think, feel, and act. Winning players and winning teams make things happen. They see themselves as being response-able or "at cause" for their success . . . as opposed to being a victim of their situation and circumstance.

An oft-cited remedy managers offer for enhancing performance is to "make their people more accountable." Tom, the CFO of a successful financial services organization, is an accountant (and marathoner). Not surprisingly, he preaches accountability to his team. Accountability implies knowing what has to be done and then performing to a specified standard. Accountability requires having a scoreboard with valid performance measures.

Tom believes accountability is a concept people often support verbally but when it actually comes to action are not always willing to pay the price. He sees a difference between accountability in sport and business. "In sport, a lack of accountability is seen almost immediately. Your check gets loose and scores. You fail to tackle the guy and he gets a touchdown. In business, accountability is often longer term and requires more complex measurement. For example, accountability for a sales target may take months to achieve, and if one does achieve it (volume) but at too low a price, the question becomes, 'Am I accountable? Is it my fault we're not profitable?' Perhaps the cause for the lack of profit was the economy turning against us, shifting margins, or a lack of support from others." Tom continued, "A lot of people refer to the fact that we have quarterly reviews as proof of their accountability.

However, when times get tough, the 'we' often turns to 'I' (like, 'I'm doing my job,' or, 'I did what was asked of me.') By contrast, in good times everyone is willing to share the glory."[3]

I recall Tom relating that fiscal accountability wasn't as sexy or captivating a goal for his financial services team as some of the other corporate challenges being discussed within the organization. I suggested he discuss with the team why fiscal responsibility was a core issue for the entire organization. How, without it, many of these other, "sexier" programs would simply not be possible. He acknowledged that it was important that his team value their contribution of providing vital big picture fiscal feedback to the organization. As he underlined the relevance of what they were doing, he reported that his staff became more enrolled in making it happen.

A similar case can be made for sweat as opposed to glory in sport. The linemen and grunts in football, and the grinders and checkers in hockey, often set the table and tone, enabling the teams' stars and scorers to excel. For a working, winning, and harmonious organization, it's important that the grinders' and grunts' contributions to team success be measured and acknowledged along with the players who score the goals and touchdowns. That is not always the case. Dave "Tiger" Williams was a tenacious checking left-winger, an NHL all star (and the most penalized player in the history of the NHL). Tiger says, "It's mentally tougher to be a good checker than it is to be a scorer. A good checker has to talk himself into doing a lousy job, one that is usually unacknowledged, and doing it well. It's often a thankless job. You can check the top snipers off the score sheet, but when it comes to negotiating next year's salary they look at who scored 30 or 40 goals, and your efforts as a checker are often forgotten."[4]

On successful teams everyone makes a difference. To be the best we can be, individually and collectively, we all need quality feedback . . . and meaningful acknowledgement.

Bottom line: Winning teams require an objective measure of performance, a scoreboard that tells them exactly how they are doing. Clear feedback, and the ability to continuously assess and adjust, are vital to team success.

Acknowledgement

Acknowledgement is another expression of feedback. It can be a powerful form of purposeful information that supports desired results. Winning teams communicate efficiently and provide positive, purposeful acknowledgement.

Effective team play can be described with a performance model consisting of a continuous loop that traces flow as follows:

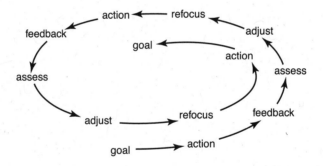

In a performance model an ongoing process of assessment and adjustment supports continuous improvement.

Positive Feedback

Winning teams provide quality feedback on team members' performances, good and bad . . . especially good. In his classic book *The One Minute Manager*, Ken Blanchard defines three keys to being a winning manager:[5]

1. set simple goals,

2. find something to praise, and

3. critique the behavior, not the person.

Simple, measurable goals are part of a team's direction and strategy, and should be a driving force and key to each player's focus. Finding something specific and goal-related to praise, and critiquing behavior and not the person, are two additional elements of successful feedback.

One key to providing winning acknowledgement is having *positive eyes* . . . and finding things to praise. It's looking for positive behavior to reinforce and encourage. Realistically, the behavior leadership is seeking is not always present. Sometimes leadership has to nurture the desirable behavior with patience and shaping. In shaping, gradual approximations of the desired behavior are reinforced, until the desired end behavior is present. Positive eyes and a positive mindset are keys to the developmental process. Selective perception is a reality. If you look for something to praise, you'll frequently find it. If you look for something to criticize, you'll usually find that too.

At the end of pro training camps, baseball and hockey teams regularly hold management meetings to evaluate personnel. They review the performance of all the players in camp to determine who will remain with the big league club, who will be released, and to which of the organization's other teams will the remainder be assigned. At one such meeting, when it was decided that a particular player was to be assigned to a minor league team, I overheard the head coach of that minor league team make several negative remarks about the player. After the meeting, I chatted with the coach about the player in question. I saw him as talented and hard-working. However, the coach saw him as a worrier and underachiever. He felt he had enough experience of the man to have formed a valid, negative opinion of him.

I couldn't argue with the coach's experience and expertise. However, I suggested that since the player was to be part of his team, instead of the coach looking to the player's perceived inadequacies (there is a tendency to look for and see what we expect), he think of him more as the player he would like him to be. Further, I suggested he actively demand these positive qualities from the player and acknowledge and reinforce that behavior when it was present. The best way to help someone to excel is to focus on the behavior we want to see manifest. Alternatively, I added, "If you keep negative eyes on him, you increase the probability that you'll see his short-comings and find things to criticize. In the end, he will be that underachiever you expected him to be."

I had a similar discussion with a sales manager regarding one of the members of his sales team. Consulting with the team, I knew the saleswoman in question to be bright and motivated. She was also someone who wanted to please and was very responsive to positive feedback. The sales manager, however, was a practical numbers person who felt she was a low producer who was wasting his time. I asked him what specific behaviors he wanted to encourage in her. He thought for a while and then listed several specific actions he thought could make her more successful. I acknowledged his analysis and suggested that rather than expecting less from her, he look at her with a positive mindset and go out of his way to shape and acknowledge her efforts, particularly in regard to the behaviors in question.

I agree with the dictum that to help people reach their full potential, catch them doing something right. Many coaches and leaders don't look aggressively enough for things to praise. Cliff, a seventeen-year veteran of professional sport and a solid team player, once said to me, "I do six things right and one thing wrong, and what feedback do I get? Criticism for the one thing I did that was wrong. That's not motivating and it's not smart."[6]

People want to be appreciated. Most are very responsive to honest, positive feedback. When the feedback is excessively negative and critical, performance can suffer.

Following a dominating first period in the Swiss Elite hockey league that ended with the home team leading 4–1, I was surprised to witness their coach come into the dressing room and blast his players for the one goal they gave up. Following the tirade, the team gave up five more goals and ended up losing the game 6–5 (to an inferior team that hadn't beaten them at home in close to a decade). Later, I discussed with the coach his decision to be highly critical of the team after a very positive effort in the first period. His explanation was, "I didn't want us to become complacent." Hindsight is 20/20, and a little more positive acknowledgment may have had a much more productive impact.

Following a disappointing performance, when the people clearly know their performance was below standard, it can be effective to say, "That is not acceptable. That's not who we are," and then focus on the *positive*. However, in my experience coaches and managers rarely take that approach. The tendency is to criticize and focus on the negative.

At an international tournament a World Cup team easily won its first three games, outscoring the opposition 13–2. In their fourth game against a formidable opponent they were soundly beaten 4–0. Following the loss the coach, a very tactically minded individual (more T than F . . . see Chapter 3) was highly critical of the team. Instead of reviewing their performance with a "that's not who we are" approach, then focusing on what the team could and should do to be more effective, he was highly critical of the players. He absolved himself of responsibility for the loss, telling the players the game plan was right and it was their incompetence and lack of commitment that caused the loss. The result was that the players became more tentative and less confident . . . and lost their next match to an inferior team.

In contrast, Dave, an NHL veteran, related an experience he had while playing with the New York Islanders. Following a game in which the Islanders played poorly and lost 5–0, the team flew to Toronto, where they were scheduled to play their next game. When they arrived at their hotel and checked in at about 1 a.m., they were told there was a meeting scheduled in the coach's suite in a half hour (at 1:30 in the morning). Dave said the players were tired and not looking forward to the prospect of being criticized for a really poor performance. However, when they arrived at the meeting, they were pleasantly surprised to find a buffet spread and cold beer, and then hear the coach say, "Men, that was a horseshit performance. That's simply not who we are. We didn't play our game. Let's forget about it. *We'll be better tomorrow.* Now, let's have something to eat, and a beer, and tell a few stories." The players appreciated the consideration and responded by bouncing back in their next game and soundly beating the Toronto Maple Leafs.

That's not to suggest in any way that we should ignore or fail to acknowledge poor performance. *Not at all!* Winning teams must establish a standard of excellence. It's a vital part of their identity. Winning leadership should be unwavering about demanding that level of performance from team members. Good performance is reinforced. Poor performance is unacceptable. When performance is substandard, the feedback should be clear and focused on the behavior; "That's not good enough. That's not who we are." Then, frame it in the positive. "Who you/we are is_____." Again, highlight what is positive, what is expected, and what is possible.

There is little value in feedback that expresses intense, negative emotion and berates the individual. One coach I worked with consistently swore at his players. After a while, a number of his players lost respect and tuned him out. As one veteran player put it, "Does he really think swearing at us helps us to perform better?" Sadly, there are countless examples of individuals who have been negatively impacted by thoughtless criticism. Gary, a veteran pro player with a fifteen-year career, acquired the nickname "F-ckin'" early in his career, because the coach consistently used the F word to preface his name. When I discussed the nickname with Gary he said, "The guys may have thought it was amusing but there was no pleasure coming to work each day and knowing what I was in for. I had a knot in my gut all the time I was there. It was only after I was traded that I really felt appreciated and began to play well."

In discussing effective leadership and emotional intelligence, Daniel Goleman underlines the importance of self-awareness, self-regulation, and empathy.[7] These qualities are most relevant and most challenged under pressure.

I remember standing on the sideline in an NFL game when a defensive back made a thoughtless mistake. When he came off the field, the coach yelled at him, "Are you stupid? What the f—did you do that for?" Truth is, the coach didn't want to know why the player did what he had done. What he really wanted to do was underline the appropriate and desired interpretation and reaction. What would have been more helpful is saying something like, "When they come out in _____ formation your responsibility is_____. Have you got it? Good. Then do it!" Self-awareness, self-regulation, empathy, and effective communication can be enhanced with training.

Over the years, at times I have observed anxious, frustrated, and embarrassed coaches venting and putting players down. Instead of projecting the image of the behavior they are looking for, they are telling the talent they are stupid, incompetent, and underlining the very behavior they want to avoid. The occasional emotional outburst can certainly capture attention and be a wake-up call for what is unacceptable. However, in general, repeated negative, emotional venting is purposeless and undermines confidence and winning.

Several years ago I was speaking to the St. Louis Blues, a successful NHL team that was filled with numerous veterans and future Hall of Fame players. I spoke about the importance of knowing your job and having a clear positive focus both for mental preparation and building confidence. After the talk, one of the players approached me and explained he had several different roles on the team and at times he wasn't sure what he should be doing. I said to him, "You are an intelligent professional athlete and it's important to be clear about your role and what is expected of you. Indeed, you should be clear enough that you can actually visualize yourself doing it. It should be part of your mental preparation before games." I went on to say, "I understand your confusion. However, I am not the coach. It's not for me to say what you should be doing. You're an intelligent guy. You must talk to the coach and get clear about your exact role and what's expected." The player agreed to speak to the coach, and left. Immediately after, the coach, Roger Neilson, came over with a big smile on his face. "What's so amusing, Rog?" I asked.

"I think it's the first time that anyone ever called him intelligent," he replied with a chuckle.[8]

"Well," I said, "If you want him to play intelligently maybe you should tell him he is intelligent." Labeling people as intelligent is a tenet I use repeatedly in my "coaching." Too frequently, we are critical of people and their performance instead of raising expectation and self-esteem with positive acknowledgement.

Praise does wonders for our sense of hearing.
—Arnold Glasgow[9]

Bill Russell, in his book, *Russell Rules*,[10] relates some advice a CEO passed on to him regarding acknowledgement and coaching success:

- Remember the five most important words: "I am proud of you."

- Remember the four most important words: "What is your opinion?"

- Remember the three most important words: "I appreciate that."

- Remember the two most important words: "Thank you."

- Remember the most important word: "You."

In a rather bizarre piece of research, Cleve Backster demonstrated that even *plants* respond favorably to praise.[11] Backster's research over twenty years ago found that plants that were repeatedly praised grew significantly taller then plants that were threatened. Philodendrons aside, the evidence suggests that positive reinforcement leads to more consistently favorable performance than negative feedback. Most experts suggest that *the ratio of positive to negative feedback should be three or four to one.*

Acknowledgement nurtures performance and well-being. At the individual level, it's important for people to be acknowledged. However, it is equally important for people to learn to acknowledge themselves for performing well. One of the most common performance flaws that people make is not acknowledging their good performance, but rather to focus on, energize, and deprecate themselves for their negative performance. Ultimately, that undermines confidence. This issue is discussed more fully when we explore the importance of identity and self-image in Chapter 9.

Winning teams set a standard. They demand excellence and they acknowledge and reinforce good performance. They highlight poor performance as unacceptable, reframe it in terms of a positive expectation . . . and demand more.

EVALUATE:

How does your team keep score?

What are the performance/success measures for your team?

How are you performing?

How do you measure your personal performance?

How is your personal performance measured by others?

On a scale of 1–10 rate the objectivity and accuracy of the feedback you are experiencing within the organization.

1 2 3 4 5 6 7 8 9 10
poor   excellent

Is there some form of feedback that you are currently not experiencing that would help you to perform more effectively?

Acknowledgement:

How clear are you about the job you are expected to perform?

1 2 3 4 5 6 7 8 9 10
unclear   extremely clear

How consistently are you acknowledged for performing well?

1 2 3 4 5 6 7 8 9 10
never   all the time

How consistently do you acknowledge yourself for performing well?

1 2 3 4 5 6 7 8 9 10
never   all the time

CHAPTER 7

CONFIDENCE

*Winning teams **believe** they can. They expect to win.*

The performance question I'm most frequently asked (along with "How can I improve my golf game?") is "What can I do to increase my confidence?"

Two things build confidence: success and preparation.

Success

One evening I received a phone call from the coach of an NHL hockey team. The team had been performing poorly and had just suffered another disappointing loss. The coach called from the team plane on the flight back home to ask, "Can you be at the arena tomorrow afternoon at 2 p.m.? I'd like you to talk to the team about confidence." When I arrived the following afternoon, the team was assembled in the dressing room. I began the meeting by asking the players, "What builds confidence?" The room was silent. After about thirty seconds the captain, Mark Messier, replied, "Winning . . . success."

Of course Mark's right. Nothing builds confidence like performing well. In any field, knowing what to do, and being able to do it successfully, is the single greatest lift to a person's confidence. Football great

Y.A. Tittle has said, "You have to have a past history of some success to give yourself status and self confidence. You have to have accomplished something before you can believe in yourself."[1]

Preparation

Winning builds a winning expectation. At the individual or team level, success says, "I can," and strengthens your belief system more than any other experience. But what if you're not experiencing success? Or what if you haven't been successful at this level before? What else could strengthen feelings of confidence? Preparation.

Winning coaches emphasize the importance of preparation. Vince Lombardi said, "Confidence comes from planning and practicing well. Get ready during the week, and the confidence will be there on Sunday. This confidence is a difficult thing to explain. But you do get it and the team gets it, if you prepare properly."[2] Bobby Knight, the legendary basketball coach, said, "The will to succeed is important, but what's more important is the will to prepare."[3]

Confidence-building preparation involves four things:

- First, it's knowing your job. It's knowing the specifics of what has to be done to succeed. On winning teams the players are coached to understand their role and the specific behaviors or 'elements' that go into making success possible. Knowing what is expected and knowing how to do it form the basis of knowing that you can.

Confidence also evolves out of improving skills: mental, physical, and technical skills.

Skills are developed through practice. Proper preparation includes practicing everything, from exercising the specific skill sets involved in performing the tasks required, to simulating effective reactions to a variety of challenging performance situations, both in imagination and in real life.

Roger Staubach, a Hall of Fame quarterback with the Dallas Cowboys, who became a successful real estate magnate, says, "The most important thing is preparation. You have to do everything you can to be successful. As an athlete I really worked hard to be ready for the moment. When the moment came I had paid the price. It's the same in business. You work hard to prepare yourself. It takes a lot of unspectacular preparation to get spectacular results."[4]

In Formula 1 racing, less time means more money and more success. It may be hard to believe that during a pit stop a top Formula 1 racing team can change the four wheels of a racing car in less then 3 seconds. They can do that and refuel the car (pumping in over 50 liters of fuel) in less than seven seconds.[5] That's simply amazing. The key to their success is practiced teamwork. The twenty-plus crew members rehearse and practice the pit stop 1500 to 2000 times a year. And they watch videos of their process, practicing and practicing some more until they are confident that they are as smooth and fast as can be . . . and that they can consistently perform well under pressure.

- Confidence comes from being healthy. I had a call from Matt, a professional athlete who was rehabilitating following a post-season hip surgery. His recovery was progressing slowly and he expressed some concerns regarding his readiness for the upcoming season. He said, "I'm just not feeling as confident as I would like to be." I explained to Matt that preparation builds confidence, and that he simply wasn't physically prepared to perform at his best. The good news was that he had time to heal and that he was enrolled in what appeared to be a well-supervised rehab program.

I encouraged him to work at his program and with time he would feel stronger, better prepared . . . and ultimately more confident.

Being healthy and in shape may apply directly to sport; however, it finds expression in business as well. When I surveyed 100 successful corporate leaders as to the single non-business factor that could most limit their personal and team success, their response was ill health. If you want to kick-start an excellent season in sales or service, or manage your team with more impact and ease, one place to begin is with a sensible program of regular exercise and a healthy diet. Respecting yourself is a step to gaining the respect of others. (Health affects the bottom line. Estimates are that $300 billion is spent annually by employers in the USA on worker absenteeism, lower productivity, turnovers, and direct medical, legal, and insurance costs.)

- Along with knowing the job and task mastery, confidence is about "feeling right." The way we are "wired" as human beings, our feelings affect our thinking and our thinking, in turn, affects our feelings.

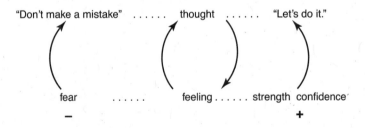

"Right feeling" comes from having the mental skills and emotional control to prepare properly and to deal with the intense feelings generated by the pressure of competition. Being in control, or, as they say in baseball, being in command, requires a special set of psychological skills, skills that can be strengthened with training. Learning to control emotions is a confidence builder that can lead to significant performance increments.

One of my young clients, a goalie, e-mailed me the following message after returning home from a tournament. "Hi, Dr. Miller—I just got back from the IDT tournament . . . I played very well all through the tournament, though I did have some shaky moments. When these moments occurred I went back to my breathing, remembered my ABC's and was fine from then on."[6] Managing the shaky moments builds confidence. Conversely, not having emotional control can lead to inconsistency, disappointing performance decrements, and a lack of confidence.

Anxiety causes tension and dis-ease. Anxious feelings erode confidence. Of course, some people feel anxious even when well-prepared. However, feelings affect thinking. To be a positive, confident thinker you must control your emotions. It's difficult to think positive, confident, power thoughts when your heart is racing, breathing is shallow, and a voice somewhere in the background of your consciousness is whispering, "Don't screw up." Confidence evolves out of learning how to transform the physical feelings of tension and dis-ease into psychophysical feelings of ease and power.

The central human emotions are love and fear. People can perform well with fear, but over the long haul performing in such a state of dis-ease creates vulnerability, a tendency to break down, and disease itself. In contrast, people who love the game and embrace the challenge they are facing are energized. They create a context for excellence. To improve performance, bring more love to your process. To generate positive feelings and strengthen confidence, I spend a considerable amount of time with all kinds of performers (elite athletes, corporate executives, surgeons, dentists, sales managers, professional coaches, police officers, musicians, actors, artists, and writers) working with them on conscious breathing to enhance their power and focus.

Conscious Breathing

"Breath is life . . . and power"

A major part of creating the right feeling is learning how to breathe consciously. Conscious breathing does three things.

1. It connects mind and body. When people are nervous (fearful), they frequently experience racing thoughts. It's as though their mind is going 80 mph and their body is doing 5 mph. This disintegration feels uncomfortable, produces more anxiety, and undermines confidence. In contrast, relaxed, rhythmical breathing is integrating.

2. Anxious thinking is characterized by worrisome, negative thoughts of the past ("Why did I _____, or why didn't I do _____.") or worrisome, negative thoughts of the future. ("What will happen if _____.") Focusing on breathing brings you back to the present. That's where the power is. The game is played in the present. As you experience the breath, the thought is "There is only this breath . . . . Now, there is only this breath . . . ."

3. When people are anxious, they often focus on things over which they have little or no control. Focusing instead on your breathing (especially on drawing in energy with each inhalation) brings a sense of energy, competence, power, and self-control back to the breather . . . all of which builds confidence.

A principle worth remembering is that *people tend to perform under pressure as they have previously performed under pressure in the past.* People who have experienced great tension during significant competitive challenges in the past will tend to get uptight before most big games or competitive challenges in the future, unless they over-train themselves to be comfortable at a lower level of emotional intensity. In other words, to break a habit of feeling tense and contracted under pressure you have

THE ABCs OF BREATHING

I coach my clients to cue three things in the breathing.

The first is rhythm—feeling or experiencing the breath flowing in and feeling or experiencing the breath flowing out. The breath is like waves in the ocean, continuously flowing in and out.

To balance and recharge, I encourage clients to take the time (even if it's only five minutes a day) to experience their natural breathing rhythm. There's power in rhythm.

The second breathing cue involves bringing a little more awareness to the in-breath. I remind my clients that if breathing is respiration, then the in-breath is the inspiration. A part of effective preparation is inspiring one's self. We can do that by being conscious of drawing energy to us with each in-breath.

The third breathing focus is direction. It is about directing the energy we breathe in, first internally, through the body; into the hands, the feet, and head, like a five-pointed star. I encourage clients to allow themselves to "imagine energy flowing to you and through you." The idea is to feel powerful.

You can also direct your energy externally, into whatever you are working to achieve. For example, a pitcher takes an inanimate object (a baseball) and, by directing his energy, sends it out to the desired target. Similarly, a salesperson directs his or her energy out in pitching a concept to a prospective buyer.

At first, conscious breathing may seem awkward, but with relatively little practice, you can generate feelings of ease and power. These feelings provide a basis for effective mental preparation and build confidence.

to practice creating feelings of ease in low-arousal, non-challenging situations. That can be accomplished by practicing relaxed, rhythmical breathing for a few minutes every day in non-threatening situations. Over time, the new feelings of ease and power generated by the breathing process will become a firmly established habit. As they do, it becomes easier to experience a greater sense of ease and power going into pressure situations . . . and both confidence and performance will improve.

Glen was a professional athlete who vomited before every game. It was an unnecessary and unattractive stress behavior that didn't in any way enhance his performance. Glen was referred to me for counseling by the team physician. After two sessions of relaxed breathing Glen's anxious pre-game ritual ceased. He felt more comfortable and played well. A sidebar to the story that illustrates how players on a team are inter-connected is that after Glen stopped his pre-game vomiting, one of his teammates said to me, "I'm glad you helped him with that. Watching him throw up in a towel before the game didn't exactly increase my confidence and get me ready to play."

Confidence comes from the root word to trust. Teams that play with confidence trust in themselves and trust in each other. Preparation is a key to building a sense of trust, and the belief that working together will lead to success.

Two of football's most successful coaches have highlighted the importance of preparation in building confidence—and winning. Don Shula, one of the winningest coaches in the history of the National Football League, has an acronym to explain team success.[7] It is the word "COACH," and in essence it's about effective preparation and the confidence preparation engenders.

- The **C** stands for conviction. First of all, one must believe. The affirmation is, "I can." Indeed, this C is an affirmation of response-ability and capability.

- The **O** in coach stands for over-learning. It's the state of being so well-practiced that everyone on the team knows exactly what to do and how to do it.

- The **A** stands for audible-ready. Again, that means being so practiced and prepared that team members can read, flex, and adjust effectively to any situation you may have to face.

- The second **C** stands for consistency. Another quality of a well-prepared organization is that they are reliably effective and that they can perform well again, again, and again.

- Last, the **H** stands for honesty and an honest effort. The core of Shula's philosophy, the OAC in COACH is all about preparation. Preparation builds confidence and an expectation of success and then success itself.

Bill Parcells is another very successful leader who has repeatedly transformed losing teams into winners in one of the most competitive forums of human endeavor. Parcells believes preparedness is the key to success.[8] He has said, "We don't want our players to think during a game, because thinking takes too long. We want them to react—to have the correct moves so ingrained in practice that instinct guides them to the right place at the right time." He adds, "The more you prepare beforehand, the more relaxed and creative and effective you'll be when it counts."

Parcells feels that people perform most reliably when they're sure they can handle the task at hand, and that sureness only comes with specific preparation. He adds, "The road to execution is paved by repetition. Repetition equals preparedness, consistency, the ability to read and react." Repetition builds strength. Repetition builds confidence.

In his book *Sacred Hoops*, Phil Jackson, an NBA coach, whose teams won a remarkable nine NBA championships, noted that a turning point for the Chicago Bulls in becoming a championship team was when their superstar player, Michael Jordan, realized that the great player is the one who makes the players around him better.[9] Part of the process of improving team performance is team leaders expressing confidence in the personnel around them. This is especially true in flow games like basketball, where confidence in others is expressed by passing teammates the ball, creating scoring opportunities with them. In the corporate world confidence is also expressed in providing opportunities to teammates and setting them up to score . . . only it's usually referred to as delegation and synergy.

One challenge I've run into on occasion is a manager who is reluctant to delegate. Sometimes it's because they are anxious about entrusting others with responsibility, fearing the job won't get done. Sometimes they don't want to showcase someone else's competence or reveal that the job can be done without them. In any case, that lack of trust in themselves and others undermines confidence and team chemistry.

Preparation enhances trust. And preparation and trust build confidence and an expectation of success. Teams with confidence believe they can perform and succeed. They expect to win . . . and they do. And their success breeds more confidence, greater expectation, and still more success.

EVALUATE:

On a scale of 1–10 rate what you perceive to be the average level of confidence of team members within the organization.

1 2 3 4 5 6 7 8 9 10
low   high

On a scale of 1–10 please rate *your* present level of confidence within the team.

1 2 3 4 5 6 7 8 9 10
low   high

We've said that preparation builds confidence and that four areas of preparation are knowing your job, being healthy, improving your skills and "feeling right." Consider your current level of preparedness in each of these areas.

List specific actions that can be taken to improve in each area.

Knowing your job:

Being healthy:

Improving your skills:

Feeling right:

Create an action statement as to what you can do to improve your personal confidence on the job. Be practical and clear. "Starting tomorrow I will _____
_____."

CHAPTER 8

CHEMISTRY

The players on a winning team respect each other.

Winning? It's because the players love each other.
—NFL coach

In the mix of personalities and talent that make up an organization, good chemistry is that positive energy and support that flows between team members. Does chemistry grow out of the team's success, or is the chemistry a factor that creates team success? The answer is usually both. Interviewed after some success, players on winning teams are inclined to say, "I couldn't have done it without the support of the rest of the team." Losers, when asked, sometimes look around, and say something that represents the lack of integration or harmony of the group: "Well, I'm doing *my* job."

Three things contributing to good team chemistry are: respect/ love, selfless action, and trust. When Vince Lombardi was asked why teams win, the third reason he cited was that "the players love one another."[1] Lombardi's response doesn't refer to sentiment or affection. It doesn't mean the players even have to like each other. (Sometimes they don't.) Rather, what Lombardi meant is that on winning teams the players *respect* each other, and specifically what each contributes to the team effort. That respect is a feeling and a building block of team chemistry.

Scott Mellanby, a twenty-year veteran NHL hockey player, summed up the importance of respect in building a winning team like this: "Respect is vital. I've been an all-star and a fourth-liner. I know how it feels when the stars and first line players show respect for the rookies and fourth-line guys and make them feel an important part of the team. If your top guys believe in those players it will be easier for them to believe in themselves. And it's those third- and fourth-line guys that have to score for you in the playoffs for you to win."[2]

Scott mentioned that sometimes in practice, a star and a fringe player are paired doing drills. He added it's important for the star to make the fringe player feel he believes in his ability and to be positive, and work hard with him. He said, "I've seen first-liners who do that . . . and then there are those head hangers who send the message, 'You are not good enough to drill with me.' That kind of thing has a real negative impact on a team."

Mark Messier, a perennial NHL all-star and Hall of Fame player, earned the reputation of being a great team leader. (There's now an NHL trophy that bears his name awarded to the player who best exemplifies leadership.) According to him, "If everybody can find a way to put their personal agendas aside for the benefit of the team, they will gain for themselves in the long run. But what often happens is that people think they have to take care of themselves first and the team second. Then the infrastructure breaks down and nobody's accountable. You have to sacrifice yourself for the good of the team, no matter what role you play on the team, whether you're playing thirty minutes or two minutes a game."[3]

Davey Johnson has been one of baseball's more successful managers. As a manager he's won over a thousand games, was American

League manager of the year, and led the New York Mets to a World Series victory. When I asked Davey why teams win, he replied, "That's easy. It's chemistry." He went on to explain, "There are 25 guys on a baseball team. You don't win with 17, 14, or 10; you win with all 25 of them. All 25 players have to contribute. Each player has to feel he has a role, some job that he can perform that we are counting on, that he can prepare for. When 25 guys feel like they have a part in this team, they prepare better, they don't have to be told to get ready. They get ready mentally and physically. When this happens, and when there's no real weakness on the team, you'll win."

Davey continued, "It's the same with any sport, or in business. Competition improves chemistry. If a player performs and contributes, he feels valued. Even in smaller roles with less time, when the opportunity is there, perform, contribute and improve . . . and you'll get more time. Get all the players involved, and you'll have good chemistry. Play a lot of guys and everybody feels a part of the team. There's preparation and anticipation. All of a sudden twenty-five guys are paying attention. They're preparing without me having to say anything. That's a lot better than nine players and maybe three or four other guys being involved. Total team involvement is good chemistry."[4]

"Trust is vital to building chemistry," he added. "If I as a manager say something and don't back it up, then there's no trust. What's destructive is saying, 'I value you. Your role is this,' and then 'this' doesn't happen. My advice is, use people properly and let them do the job; that's real communication. And that builds trust and good team chemistry."

Chemistry doesn't just happen. One of several incidents where I observed Davey building trust with his players was in Los Angeles. In a game against the Dodgers, Darryl Strawberry, a star outfielder with the New York Mets, looked at a called third strike and then began to argue the call with the home plate umpire. Davey ran out on to the field, moved Darryl aside and took up his cause arguing the call with the umpire . . . for which he was ultimately thrown out of the game. Afterwards, when we discussed the incident, he said even though he knew that he could be ejected from the game (you can't argue balls and strikes), he saw it as an important opportunity to build trust with Darryl and to illustrate to him and the rest of the team that he would stand up for his players.

Just as trust in leadership is basic to commitment, trust is also a key component of good chemistry. To bond together, players need to trust leadership . . . and each other. Leadership can nurture good chemistry, encourage bonding and a surrendering of ego, and the individual "I" for the collective "we."

Without a shared commitment to serve and perform to the best of a person's ability, trust is lost, disengagement between team members occurs, and chemistry and impact are adversely affected.

During the past couple of years I've been retained by Manulife Financial to coach several of their client agencies in the area of professional excellence. In their corporate guidelines Manulife Financial stresses the importance of relationship and a team approach in developing a successful partnership between the firm and the client agencies they deal with.

After a highly profitable year, I was discussing the team process with Nadira, a Manulife Financial marketing director. I specifically asked how she saw Manulife's team orientation contributing to building successful relationships with their business partners. Nadira explained that within her team there is a collective commitment to excellence and service. "Everyone is working to be the best they can be, to be bottom-line heads up, and to do whatever we can to serve the client to the best of our ability." I noted her enthusiasm and asked her what would happen if one of her teammates simply wasn't as committed as the rest. Instantly, she replied, "It wouldn't work, trust would be lost and we couldn't tolerate that."[5] As in the previous example, Nadira's remarks highlight the interconnectedness of commitment and chemistry that exists within successful organizations.

Clay, a GM sales manager, discussed the importance of team chemistry in building a cohesive sales unit even in the "me oriented" dealership sales environment. He said, "One bad seed talking negatively on the showroom floor can have a negative impact on the group. Mindset can shift. People begin thinking about why it's difficult to sell and performance suffers. That can't be tolerated. You have to get rid of the bad seed."

In researching their book, *Performance at the Limit: Business Lessons from Formula 1 Motor Racing*, the authors (Jenkins, Pasternak, and West)[6] discovered four qualities that foster the kind of teamwork that wins races. They found that teams win when their members are doing the following:

1. sharing a clear, common goal,

2. working together to build trust between each other,

3. being willing and open to learning and collaborating, and

4. creating and working in a no-blame culture.

Each of these qualities nurtures chemistry, teamwork, and success.

The Team Retreat

Getting away from it all with the right leadership can also be a positive, chemistry-building experience. (See Chapter 12). To enhance team bonding, Coach Herb Brooks sequestered the USA "Miracle on Ice" team[7] before their remarkable Olympic gold medal performance.

A different but an equally performance-enhancing sequestering of the famous All Blacks rugby team of 1905 (nicknamed "the Invincibles") was described in Lloyd Jones's book, *The Book of Fame*.[8] In that case, the isolation of a ten-week-long ocean voyage and the creative leadership of their manager, George Dixon, who used imagery and personal sharing to connect a disparate group of men in heart and mind, supported their coming together and developing a unique and revolutionary style of play.

In some circumstances poor leadership can be a force that promotes bonding but inhibits chemistry. I have consulted with business and sport teams where leadership was inappropriate and where the group bonded together *against* what they perceived as a tyrannical or ineffective leader. In these cases the group can be tight but ultimately the chemistry of the organization as a whole was weakened and undermined by the mistrust of leadership.

Bret Hedican, a veteran pro athlete, Olympian, and solid team player, introduced another aspect of chemistry to explain why teams win. He said, "It's because of heart. A winning team is like a beating heart that keeps pumping no matter what. If the team is ahead, there's no easing. If they are behind there's no panic. The heart of the team just keeps pumping away. And the heart is really the core group of guys who set a positive rhythm that spreads out to all the players."[9] Bret described being traded from a losing team that didn't have this core heartbeat to a winning team (which won the Stanley Cup) where everyone worked together no matter what. He said, "When you came to that winning team, you just picked up the beat."

Along with the team heartbeat that Hedican describes, there are remarkable examples of people actually affecting each other's physiology and psychology. One of the most concrete examples is the McClintock effect,[10] which describes a phenomenon wherein the menstrual cycles of women living and working together tend to synchronize. There are also numerous anecdotes of people closely aligned (parent-child, twins, spouses) yet living apart sharing strong synchronous experiences.

Chemistry is real. Though *team chemistry* usually refers to a positive flow of energy between team members, chemistry between people can also be a negative or toxic force adversely affecting performance and well-being.

While good chemistry is a quality of winning teams, that's not to say there is always ease and harmony within winning teams. Just as a little spice can transform a recipe into something special, challenge, debate, and even confrontation can enrich chemistry and enhance performance. . . . but only if it comes with a respect for the team first. I've been present at both business and sport leadership meetings during which people have argued intensely about ideas behind closed doors. Often these interactions are synergistic. The bottom line is when agreement is reached and the final decisions are made, team members emerge positive and genuinely committed to the task at hand.

The era of the rugged individual is giving way to the era of the team player. Everyone is needed, but no one is necessary.
—Bruce Coslett, NFL Coach[11]

Bill Bradley, a member of NBA championship teams who has served in the US Senate said, "Championships are not won unless a team has forged a high degree of unity, attainable only through the selflessness of each of its players.[12]" Bradley went on to say that the society we live in glorifies individualism. "Basketball (and most team sports), teaches a different lesson. It's a lesson that untrammeled individualism destroys the chance for achieving success. What any one player can do alone will never equal what a team can do together." Bradley's message is becoming increasingly important in these times of "me first."

Danny Ainge, former NBA all-star, now the Boston Celtics' executive director of basketball operations, referred to chemistry when asked to explain the team's resurgence to championship form.[13] Specifically, Ainge echoed Bradley's comments citing mutual respect, selflessness, and willingness of the team's top players to share the ball and the glory, as reasons for the team's success.

Prolonged success demands a culture where individual team members respect and support each other. Leadership has a key role in nurturing a supportive context. The qualities of trust and mutual support are primal and keys to any viable social organization.

Some years ago, while studying social behavior patterns, I observed a colony of chimps in a large fenced-in jungle enclosure. The psychologist conducting the research placed a stuffed tiger in a cave in the chimps' enclosure. Using a remote device, he was able to press a button and have the tiger slide out of the cave (on a track) into the center of the enclosure. Initially, the chimps were calmly going about their daily activities, socializing, grooming, and eating. The tiger's sudden appearance caused the chimps to panic. They became agitated, shrieked, ran about chaotically. After a few minutes, as the tiger didn't move, their arousal level diminished and they began to reorganize. In the process they gathered together, slowly approaching the motionless, stuffed tiger. What followed was perhaps the most interesting observation for me.

As they inched toward the tiger, the chimps repeatedly reached out to touch each other (hand to hand or hand to shoulder). It was a way of saying or confirming, "We're all here. Right? We're in this together." The presence and support of other group members bolstered their confidence and courage. Eventually, one of the approaching chimps (supported by his peers) summoned enough courage to hit the stuffed tiger with a stick. As he did, the chimps again became agitated, shrieked, and ran back to safety. However, when the tiger didn't react, the chimps reorganized. They gathered together and began to slowly move toward the tiger. As they moved closer to the feared object, they repeatedly touched (stayed in touch with) each other.

I've observed a similar "touching behavior" in teams under pressure and stress, and also when celebrating things going well. Players on supportive teams, teams with good chemistry, reach out to teammates (verbally and physically) to acknowledge them and let them know they are with them and for them. When challenged with threat or pressure, the support of the group gives the individual team members, in all walks of life, the strength and courage to persevere.

While doing a team-building conference for a global telecommunications corporation, I was asked by one of the executives how she could improve chemistry when her team is spread all over North America. My answer was, "a little more slowly and with a little more effort." Increasingly, corporate teams are operating in a virtual reality, spread all over the country and the planet, where it is simply harder to stay in touch in the most basic ways. Sure, with the Internet and cell phones there is instant voice communication; however, without eye contact and real proximity, more time, patience, and a conscious effort are required to build trust, which is a key component of good chemistry.

The Law of the Jungle

I was called in to consult with a team that was in a single-game sudden death playoff situation. The team had to win to survive. The team they were facing in the playoff had beaten them decisively on a couple of occasions during the regular season. Luke, the coach, a former NHL star, related that his players lacked confidence and didn't think they could win. He asked for my help to get them out of their losing mindset.

To restore confidence it was important to summon their pride and generate some enthusiasm and positive chemistry. In a sit-down meeting I explained to the team that humans are remarkable beings possessing the qualities of both animals and angels. An angelic-like quality we possess as humans is our ability to imagine something and then work to make it a reality. For example, we visualize a house we would like to live in, draw a picture of it, create the blueprint, buy the materials, build it . . . and it becomes a reality. Similarly, we can think of what it would take to excel in a particular role in business or sport and then commit to doing the necessary training to make it happen . . . and then it manifests.

In contrast, getting in touch with our animal nature gives us energy, intensity, and real physical power. I often ask clients to pick an animal that would give them the qualities that would help them to meet the challenge they are facing. This group chose the wolf. I described the power of a wolf pack hunting together: their primordial drive, their intense focus, and the absence of any negative judgment. I talked about how the presence of the pack gives each wolf strength, and how wolves support each other in the hunt. We related all of this to the challenge the players were facing and how they could translate an intense wolf pack mentality into action (checking, defending, attacking, passing, scoring) and "hunting" in the game they would be playing that evening.

To highlight the point of team strength, respect, and support, I recited a poem of Rudyard Kipling's, one I have repeated to corporate and sport teams alike on numerous occasions:

And this is the law of the jungle.
As old and as true as the sky.
And the wolves that keep it will prosper
And the wolves that break it must die.

As the creeper girdles the tree trunk
This law runs forward and back,
The strength of the pack is the wolf
And the strength of the wolf is the pack.[14]

The players responded positively. Their energy and enthusiasm grew. They became excited about the challenge they faced together. That evening they hunted *together* like a pack of wolves, and won the game . . . advancing to the next round of the playoffs.

Chemistry is the mortar that binds the bricks together.

Chemistry is a feeling. That feeling evolves in the shared commitment people have performing and competing alongside each other in meaningful pursuits.

Chemistry is feeling a part of the solution. It is expressed in respect for teammates and what each contributes. Chemistry is about everyone contributing. Winning chemistry occurs when the "we" is bigger and more important than "me." Winning chemistry is about selflessness, sacrifice, and support. Winning teams have chemistry.

EVALUATE:

In regard to mutual respect and trust, how would you rate team chemistry in your organization?

1 2 3 4 5 6 7 8 9 10

poor   excellent

Everyone makes a difference. List three things you can do you do personally to improve team chemistry. Be specific.

Take a moment to write down any additional thoughts or suggestions on improving team chemistry:

CHAPTER 9

IDENTITY

Winning teams define themselves by a standard of excellence.

A team's identity is one of the most important ingredients in winning.
—Scotty Bowman, the winningest coach in NHL history[1]

Identity is self-image. It's who you think you are. At any level, individual or team, who you think you are is critical to how you perform.

Some years ago, shortly after he was the first North American to win cycling's grueling Tour de France, Greg LeMond was hunting in California with his brother-in-law when he was accidentally shot at close range. Surgeons worked for over 20 hours to remove dozens of pellets from his body. LeMond was close to death. A year later he returned to racing. One of my clients was racing in Tennessee at one of LeMond's first races back. He said LeMond looked terrible, "like death warmed over"; however, when the breakaway group surged ahead of the field, there he was at the head of the pack with the handful of race leaders.

Listening to the story, I asked the group of elite cyclists I was consulting with how was it possible that LeMond, who was just getting back to competition after his harrowing near-death experience and was clearly not in top racing shape, could be with the leaders in the break-away group. The consensus of the group was simple: "That's where he thought he belonged." LeMond went on to win the Tour de France a second time.

Winning teams, like successful individuals, have a winning identity that drives them to excel. I mentioned earlier that for a number of years I ran an interdisciplinary treatment clinic. We provided an outstanding level of clinical care, and the consensus of the medical team was that in our area of specialization we had the premier program in the country. One of the therapists attended a professional conference. When she returned from the meeting she said, "Saul, if we have the best program in the country, then we have to improve our marketing package. There was a clinic at the conference doing a better job of marketing themselves than we are." I was delighted with her interest and concern. On winning teams, players take ownership and pride in being among the best, and they appreciate that they must continuously strive to maintain that level of performance.

Doug Reisborough, the general manager of the NHL Minnesota Wild hockey team, related an event reflecting a similar sense of identity.[2] Reisborough had played for the Montreal Canadiens during the years when that team was a dynasty and a perennial Stanley Cup winner. He said they were playing an expansion team at the Montreal Forum, the site where Canadiens championship teams reigned supreme. And they were losing the game 3–0 at the end of the second period. He said, "I remember the players being pissed off and saying, *that's not who we are*, to be losing to these bums. And we went out in the third period and scored a bunch of goals."[2]

Successful teams expect to perform well. The idea "That's who we are," is key to a winning team's identity. When a team performs poorly, the thought should be, "That's *not* who we are. Who we are is _____." And they should fill in the blank with the positive thought or image.

Sales, like golf, is an "I" game. To be successful, golfers and sales-people must consistently acknowledge or reinforce a positive sense of self. Watching V.J. Singh play a PGA Tournament round, I noticed that when he hit a shot that was less than perfect he didn't get notice-ably upset. Instead, he stood over an imaginary ball and took another swing, and visualized the shot going where he wanted it to go. He ap-peared to acknowledge the imaginary shot and say to himself, "That's who I am," before moving on. That positive sense of self builds consis-tency and confidence.

Successful teams and winning team members reinforce a positive identity by acknowledging their positive performances. They establish a standard of excellence that represents who they are. While talking to a group of developing athletes, I was asked by one of the adolescents if the world's best athletes have negative thoughts. "Of course they do," I replied. "The thing that differentiates them—and successful people in all fields—is that they don't focus on the negatives. Instead they focus on the positive, on what they are working to create."

Acknowledge your positive self. In my experience one of the most limiting performance habits, and something that undermines a posi-tive sense of self, is that people do not reliably acknowledge their good performance. When they perform well, they often take it for granted and think, "It's expected. It's no big deal. It's what I was sup-posed to do." When they perform poorly, when they say or do the wrong thing, they tend to focus on the negative aspects of their past performance.

Love and Fear

Fear is the great limiter. It makes us smaller. I am referring principally to the fear of failure, the fear of embarrassment, the fear of not being okay, and the fear of letting the team down. When people experience fear and anxiety, they contract psychically as well as physically, and bring to mind the possibility of failure. A team is not a vacuum. People affect each other. A negative, anxious teammate can have a contractive, limiting effect on those around them.

As I said earlier, love and fear are core human emotions. An antidote to performance anxiety (fear) and negative thinking is a strong positive sense of self. I regularly encourage clients, "Love the game and love the challenge you are facing." Love is empowering. It strengthens our sense of possibility. It makes us bigger. Performers who love the challenge gain power.

Here are three of the easiest ways to bring love to your process.

- Take time to breathe. Remember, relaxed rhythmical breathing can create feelings of ease and power. It feels good. It reminds us who we are and that we have the response-ability in the here and now to be at our best. (See Exercise 8 in Chapter 12).

- Be kind (and positive) to yourself. Saying positive things to yourself and visualizing yourself performing well strengthens your self-image.

- When you (or your teammates) do the small things that contribute to success, acknowledge and reinforce them. Say, "That's who I am," or "That's who we are." Acknowledging positive performance feels good. It builds confidence and grows a positive sense of self and team. Remember, repetition builds strength.

A team I was working with had to win a gold medal at the Pan American Games to qualify for the Olympics. Their competitive challenge was a team from Argentina who were perennial champions. As they prepared for the tournament, I noticed that one of the strikers, named Reg, was a smaller player and had acquired the nickname

"Gnome." It's not uncommon for players to bestow nicknames on teammates that are less than complimentary or empowering. I used the situation to bring to the players' attention that how we talk to each other can strengthen or weaken both our individual and collective sense of self. I explained to the players that referring to Reg as Gnome didn't give him power and instructed them to call him by his given name or find another nickname for him. Reluctantly, they complied. Perhaps it made a difference (I believe it did); maybe it was simply coincidence; but in the gold medal game, Reg scored the winning goal.

I recall discussing the team's performance with Victor, the president of the sporting association, after the team's gold medal win. He said, "You know, Saul, it wasn't that the team played so much better; it was as if they had a change of heart. I don't know what you did but they just didn't believe they would lose." What Victor was describing was a shift in the team's identity.

Whether my clients are senior executives or sales managers, or golfers, football, baseball, hockey players, I usually ask them to define what they have to do to be successful. An exercise I frequently use to strengthen their performance identity is to ask them to complete the statement, "When I perform/play my best I _____."

I instruct them to fill in the blank with specific information clear enough for them to actually visualize themselves performing these behaviors. By changing the way we look at ourselves, we can change both our performance and ourselves.

Before an important performance or event, I encourage clients to take a few moments to relax and breathe (to generate a positive, powerful, comfortable feeling . . . to love themselves), and to get in touch with who they are. I suggest they affirm themselves as capable, response-able performers who love the challenge. I encourage them to visualize themselves performing well.

I sometimes recommend that they create a power statement—a list of positive affirmations describing themselves performing confidently and effectively.

The power statement of a CFO of a highly successful financial institution who was dealing with mergers, risk management issues, and an unstable global economy could be something like this:

- I am in control.

- I project confidence.

- I have done my research and analysis.

- I understand the issue.

- We have options and solutions.

- I provide context and direction.

- Our financial strategies are robust and flexible to deal with the challenges and opportunities the markets present.

- We will succeed as our actions are thoughtful, strategic, and impactful.

- I enjoy the challenge.

- I am in control.

- I project confidence.

Similarly, the power statement an NHL veteran used on his way to winning the Stanley Cup was this:

- I am an outstanding hockey player.

- I am strong and fast, and I read the play well.

- On offense, I have the ability to make things happen.

- I see opportunities and I make excellent passes.

- I rush the puck with speed and confidence.

- I am a force when I jump into the play.

- I have a strong accurate shot.

- I love to set up and score goals.

- On defense, I always have good position.

- One-on-one I am unbeatable.

- I'm like a tiger: quick, strong, and powerful.

- Offensively and defensively I am a force.

- I prepare myself well.

- I am a team player.

- I enjoy playing this game and I am very *good at it.*

- I am an outstanding hockey player.

This kind of mental preparation strengthens self-image and is an effective antidote to negativity and performance anxiety. It increases confidence and consistency. Over the years, I have been fortunate to work with some very good teams who defined themselves in some of the following ways:

"Whatever happens, we can handle it."

"We always prevail in the end."

"An excellent place to work."

"No one outworks us."

"We're winners."

"We provide a superior quality of service."

"We are environmentally sustainable."

"We are tough."

Not surprisingly, the winners walked their talk.

Each and every team member contributes to a team's identity. The question is, how and what do they contribute? When the collective belief is "We are capable, and we can succeed" they usually will.

I was with a very good NFL Rams team in Atlanta, playing a not very good Falcons team. Though we were the better team, we were struggling in the first half, making errors, and were losing 17–0 at half time. In the dressing room players seemed surprised, confused, and negative, saying things like, "What's wrong?" and "We can't seem to get it together."

Then the coach spoke. He said, "Men, the team we are playing today are losers. They are going to give us the game. However, because of some mistakes we made in the first half we have a very limited margin of error. We can only give them three points in the second half." He continued, "We are the better team. If we stay positive and stick to our game plan, we will win this game." He paused, then repeated with a sense of confidence, "Men, they are losers. They will make mistakes. They will give us the game. Now let's go out there and *play our game*."

The effect of what the coach said was profound. It stopped all the negative chatter in the room. It was as if our team instantly remembered who we were (the superior team) and who the opposing players were ("losers"). Inspired, or reminded who they were by the coach's comments, the team went out in the second half and played like winners . . . and true to character, the opposition played like losers and gave us a chance to win the game.

I was having breakfast with Bill, a fifteen-year veteran of professional sport and a member of a team with a losing history that was struggling to become a playoff contender for the first time. I had been attempting to strengthen the team's less-than-positive identity. Bill was skeptical of some of my ideas, especially my emphasis on creating and focusing on a positive image of what the team was capable of achieving. He said, "You know, Saul, I think positive-mindedness and a positive self-image are good things, but don't you think that stuff only goes so far? What if we are not really as good as you make us out to be?"

I explained to Bill that positive-mindedness is fundamental to success. The mind leads and the body follows. *Our thoughts have a chemical expression and impact.* Positive thoughts of belief, confidence, and desire release neurochemicals in the brain that stimulate the body to respond with greater energy and power.

Repetition builds strength. Neurons that fire together wire together. When people consistently think positively they create neural networks that facilitate success. In contrast, negative thoughts, thoughts charged with worry, failure, depression, and despair also affect brain chemistry. These negative thoughts produce neurochemicals that affect body chemistry in a way that reduces energy and the likelihood of success. When an entire team wants to win, believes they can win, embraces a standard of excellence, and when the players consistently commit and work to perform to that standard in thought and action, the neurochemistry of the team shifts, their performance improves, and the team's confidence and self-images grows stronger.

A strong team identity is an antidote to pressure-induced emotional behavior. When I began working with a women's World Cup soccer team, one task I was given was to help build a positive team identity.

We focused on two key identity factors. One was, *We are a team who plays to win and knows what we have to do to succeed*. That meant defining (as mentioned in Chapter 6) specific success factors, relevant to their game. The aim was for team members to clearly understand, *When we do this, we will be successful*, and then to do the necessary training to make that happen. The other identity factor was *We are family*. When we discussed the family aspect, I asked team members to list the qualities of a healthy, functional family. They mentioned qualities like respect, trust, support, caring, commitment, and honest communication.

Traveling and competing around the world in major pressure events like the World Cup and the Olympic Games, the team's identity as winners and as family helped them sustain a high level of performance. They developed a positive, supportive winning culture, despite the inevitable challenges encountered along the way. These were just some of their challenges: players being injured or suspended, personal upsets between players, coaching criticism, selection issues, disappointing losses, upheavals with travel and accommodation, and referees making inappropriate calls. Through it all, being able to come back to an identity as a) a team that loves to win and knows what it takes to succeed, and b) a family (supportive, honest, caring), helped the team stay on a positive, productive course.

A team's positive identity can lift and sustain a group of individuals to achieve remarkable success. Or, if negative, that self-image can be an energy drain and a source of disappointment and underachievement.

I was with a Canadian men's field hockey team competing in a World Cup qualifying match in Malaysia against a talented South African team. The South Africans were winning 4–1 with just a few minutes left in the match. Remarkably, Canada scored four goals in the last five minutes to win the match. The collapse of the South African team was devastating; they didn't win another match for the rest of the tournament. Indeed, they lost several games in the final moments. As the pressure mounted late in these matches, you could just imagine the South African players thinking, "Oh, no; not again." Furthermore, the doubt engendered by these losses so affected their team's self-image that despite considerable talent they went on to be a losing team for the next couple of years.

Almost all of us want to be respected as winners and take exception when we are seen in less than a favorable light. Sometimes you can use this notion, and challenge a team's identity to spark performance. I was in Spain with a national team on a training tour that was a tune-up for the Olympic Games. After a rather lackluster performance against one of the local teams I said to the players, "You guys are the perfect guests to invite to a tournament."

"Why's that?" asked one of the players.

"You are polite, you have nice uniforms, you don't harass the guests, and you don't win the trophy." Their surly looks indicted I had struck a cord. I said, "Well then, if you don't like the image, let's do something about it. Let's be more assertive about dictating the pace of the game and play with the focus and intensity we're capable of. That's who we are."

As I've stated repeatedly, a team is more than a collection of individuals. It is a dynamic entity, a living system. One way or another, each team member continuously contributes to and shapes the team's identity. Winning teams are composed of individuals who consistently contribute to an identity that is positive, powerful, and enabling.

EVALUATE:

How would you rate the collective identity of your team, with specific regard to competence and competitiveness?

> 1 2 3 4 5 6 7 8 9 10
> poor   excellent

List any suggestions that might help to build a more positive team identity.

How would you rate your personal performance identity with specific regard to competence?

> 1 2 3 4 5 6 7 8 9 10
> poor   excellent

What identity image would you choose to give you qualities that could enhance your performance?

CHAPTER 10

CHARACTER AND A WINNING FORMULA

Winning teams have a nine key character.

People often refer to winning teams and winning players as having character. What is character? The Oxford dictionary defines character as "all those qualities that make a person, group, or thing what he, she, and it is, and different from others." As such, it's a collection of the nine key characteristics we've described. Remember that these nine keys are not independent entities; they are interactive, interwoven threads comprising the fabric of a winning team. They affect and contribute to each other. For example, motivation is expressed in commitment. Commitment and feedback build confidence. Motivation, commitment, feedback, and confidence support identity.

Craig, a veteran scout who has been traveling across North America for over a decade searching for the kind of talent that builds a winning team said, "The key to winning is character. It's the character of your players, especially your leaders. And a team's character is best expressed in its commitment, confidence and chemistry."[1]

Throughout the last nine chapters we have been exploring factors that build the character of a winning team. Listening to a physicist explain the difference between how atoms in a magnetized piece of metal behave, I was impressed with the similarity of his description to team behavior. He noted that atoms have a polarity and charge. In a non-magnetized piece of metal the atoms arrange themselves randomly, without direction or order. However, if that same piece of metal becomes magnetized, the atoms align themselves with their polarity and charges facing the same direction. In that manner they become an integrated, powerful, attracting (or repelling) force.

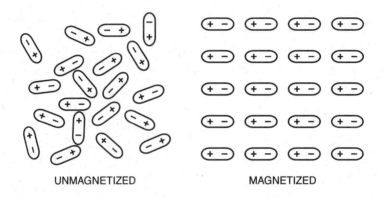

UNMAGNETIZED   MAGNETIZED

It is the same in teams, where individual team members come together, each with his or her personal wants and values, and with a unique style, and set of skills. At first their personal energies may be somewhat unfocused and multi-directional. However, with the positive integration of the keys we've discussed (purpose, talent, leadership, strategy, commitment, feedback, confidence, chemistry), a collective identity and team character emerges, and as it does, the team becomes a powerful force.

Mind, Body, Spirit

On a macro level, incorporating the nine keys of team success within the traditional trinity of mind, body, and spirit may provide an interesting perspective on the character of winning teams.

Mind

The first core quality of winning teams is directional. It's having a winning mind: a clear, positive vision and goal of what we are working towards, what we want to create . . . as well as the belief that we can achieve it. Without the belief, people are less willing and capable of investing themselves fully and expending the effort necessary to make it happen.

Intention comes from a root word *intendre*, which means "to stretch out." Winning intention involves a stretching out of the mind towards the reality we aspire to create. Winning teams create and sustain a clear, positive focus. They communicate that intention and focus to team members in mission statements, goals, and role descriptions. The players understand and appreciate the direction and can visualize their role in the collective process. They trust in the vision and in leadership. They believe they can be successful.

I have said repeatedly, "We get more of what we think about." Winning team members focus on, and take pride in, themselves and their teammates performing well. That's how winning teams think. That's who they are.

Body

The second core quality involves the doing. The talent on winning teams is a mix of personalities, skill sets, and experience, all with a unified focus. They are prepared. They know what to do, how to do it, and they are committed to doing whatever it takes to perform to the best of their ability. As I said before, commitment is the willingness to do what's necessary to accomplish one's goal. It's paying the price in effort and self-sacrifice. Winning teams pay the price.

A winning team philosophy is working hard and smart. Know the job, do the work, do it well . . . and persevere. (It's working hard and smart every interaction, every shift, every game, and every day.) How many plays decide the outcome of a football game? Often, two or three of the eighty to one hundred plays in a game are game breakers. Successful teams address the game as if each play or each transaction will make the difference between success and failure. Not in terms of tension and stress, but rather in terms of the quality and integrity of their effort.

Spirit

The third fundamental of winning teams is spirit. Spirit incorporates elements of a team's purpose, commitment, chemistry, and identity. It's the positive, creative flow of energy within and between team members. It begins with a purpose that has heart, one that captures the values of the individual and the group as a whole. It involves team members buying in, surrendering their personal "I" for the collective team "we" and working a plan together with passion.

Effective team play requires *synergy*. Synergy is about energy flow between people working together to create something more than they could create on their own. On winning teams a talented mix of personalities bond together around a common goal. The synergy that's required for the group to achieve their goal is an expression of heart. Sharing a common vision, belief, and trust is inspiring. Winning team members are inspired to excel out of respect for the mission, the team, themselves, and each other.

Teams with talent win because they integrate mind, body, and spirit in pursuit of a shared goal.

The Character of Winners and Losers: A Contrasting Study

Generally, I consult with one organization or team in a league or market at any one time. However, while putting the finishing touches on this book, circumstances presented the opportunity to work with two teams in the same league. What was especially interesting was the juxtaposition of these two teams. Team 1, a team I had worked with for several years, were winners. They had won the league championship the previous year and were again performing very well. In contrast, Team 2, based on performance, might be called losers. They had the poorest record of the twenty-plus teams in the league the previous season, and once again found themselves at the bottom of the league when I began consulting with them.

Comparing the two teams provides a brief review of the nine keys, and highlights how each element contributes to team success. In addition to my personal observations, I discussed the character of these teams with five players who had recently been traded from the winning team to the losing team, or vice versa. I believe the comparison goes beyond sport and has relevance for teams in all forms of endeavor.

- **A meaningful goal**

  The players on Team 1 had two clearly defined objectives: a team goal and a personal goal. Their team goal was for the team to be successful and win the league championship. That goal was defined for the players on the first day of training camp. In addition, each player had a personal goal, to have a successful season and to sign a lucrative professional contract. Both goals were very meaningful and motivating to the players. They were goals they could relate to and commit to achieving. Both goals were seen as possible within the current program. Individually and collectively, Team 1 members appeared energized to work diligently towards realizing both of these goals.

  For Team 2, the goal of contending for the championship was unrealistic. Players were frustrated, embarrassed, and disappointed by the team's consistently poor performance. There was disassociation from team objectives for a number of players. Indeed, most players seemed to be decidedly more focused on their individual agendas than on the team's success. Several veteran players openly expressed the desire to be traded. A couple of players voiced their frustration and unhappiness by saying that playing on such a poor team had significantly jeopardized their professional opportunities.

Suggestions: A third of the way through the new season many players on Team 2 had already written off the season. To enroll them in the team process, one suggestion was to set mini goals—scaled-down, realistic challenges they could accomplish in a brief (two- to three-game) period. To nurture personal development, I encouraged players to hold the image of the professional they were working to become and then to work diligently in practice and games to become that player.

- **Talent**

Both teams had talent. I go along with the consensus of players polled, namely, that Team 1 had better talent and greater depth than Team 2. However, we also agreed that the talent differential alone could not account for the sizable difference in team performance and results between these two teams. The talent difference that did exist could be attributed primarily to two human resource issues. Team 1 had a better scouting network. They consistently selected players that fit their performance criteria with regard to both character and skill. Team 1 also appeared to have a better program in place to develop the talent once selected. When I asked a veteran player who had been traded to Team 1 what was different about the winning team he said, "Here they select good players, not necessarily the top draft picks, but good players." He continued, "And what's really impressive is their ability to develop these players and make both them and the team better."

Team 2's selection process was flawed by weak scouting. And those talented players that were selected found themselves in a discouraging environment charged with negativity. For a number of players, their enthusiasm, work ethic, and confidence diminished over time.

Suggestions: Team 2 was encouraged to improve their selection process (and scouting network) immediately. It was suggested that management, coaching, and scouting develop clear selection guidelines based on the kind of team they wanted to develop and the type of individual they were looking for. In addition, it was suggested that team-building training be initiated to improve team culture and leadership. Again, team members were counseled to hold a long-term vision of the player they were working to become, and then strive to make it happen.

• Leadership

There were significant leadership differences between the two groups. As we have said, the head leads and the body follows. Team 1 had a well-established and effective organization in place. Coaching/top down leadership was demanding, supportive, effective, and respected. Perhaps the greatest leadership difference between the two teams was in regard to the core leadership provided by the players themselves. Within Team 1 a strong, positive, team-oriented leadership group had emerged. Collectively, this core group was purposeful, and hard-working, supportive with a winning expectation. In addition, the leadership group was appreciative about being a part of Team 1, expressing the sentiment that there was no team they would rather play for. Ongoing leadership coaching reinforced their attitude and behavior.

In contrast, Team 2's organization was in a state of flux. There were recent changes in ownership, management, scouting, and coaching. In addition, and exacerbating the problem, was the lack of solid core leadership. The losing team's leaders had no real leadership training, and because of the team's poor performance at the start of the season and in past years, the focus of the leadership group was more on themselves and their personal situation than the collective "we." Many of the leaders expressed the desire to be traded. Two messages projected by some of the veterans that resonated through the organization were "We are not a good team," and "I would rather be somewhere else."

Suggestion: You cannot assume people simply know how to lead. Two suggestions to improve Team 2's core leadership and create a culture that supports positive thinking and a committed effort were to establish leadership training for the core group, along with team-building exercises for all team members; and, if it proved impossible to get the team leaders to embrace team goals and values, then trade away some of the present negative leaders and bring in players with a more positive, winning attitude.

- **Strategy**

That is, "Know your job." Again, differences were perceived between the two groups. Team 1 members appeared to have a clear sense of what to do as defined by the team's success factors. Team 1 also understood why these success factors were important. Further, because of their success, Team 1 players believed in the system and were committed to executing according to plan.

In contrast, some of the players on Team 2 seemed unclear about strategy. Others said while there was a clear strategy in place, there was less of a consistent emphasis on execution and less accountability for not following through on it. Furthermore, with Team 2's history of losing, players were simply less trusting, confident, and dedicated to following team directives.

Suggestions: Define success factors appropriate to the current personnel. Set mini, achievable goals. Consider shaping (graduated performance steps). Acknowledge players for performing according to plan. Make players who don't perform more accountable. Use more video feedback coaching to strengthen the message. Be consistent. Consistency builds confidence.

- **Commitment**

We've said repeatedly that commitment is reflected in a willingness to do what's necessary to get the job done. It's also expressed as a surrendering of the personal "I" for the group "we." Again, the differences between Team 1 and Team 2, in regard to commitment, were significant. When asked to rate the differences between the two teams on a 10-point scale, players who played for both teams rated Team 1's commitment as 8–9 (out of 10), and Team 2's commitment as 3–4.

Team 1, with good leadership, a clear game plan, and a history of success, was a positively focused, hard-working group willing to put in the effort required to succeed. They also believed in their program, expected to win, and were willing to make the effort and ego sacrifices required for the team to be successful.

It is painful to lose. It is especially painful to give your best effort repeatedly and not be successful. Over time, losing and disappointment can lead to less buy in and less effort. Since Team 2 lacked the core leadership and belief that they would be successful, the effort they were willing to expend was inconsistent. They also appeared less motivated and less willing to sacrifice personally for the group "we" than Team 1.

Suggestions: Commitment in successful organizations often flows from the top down; it is not something that can be imposed on a group. At the rank and file level it is the product of motivation, a sense of purpose, trust in leadership, strategy, and an expectation of success. To strengthen commitment, each of those elements has to be improved. Again, the recommended approach involved improving player selection, redefining goals and strategy, setting achievable mini goals, shaping success, increasing accountability, challenging and acknowledging performance, instituting core leadership training, doing more team-building, and working to recreate a culture where players take pride in playing for each other.

• **Feedback**

The ability to assess and adjust is vital for team development and for consistent high-level performance. Feedback provides the input for making necessary adjustments.

Team 1 had several feedback indicators to evaluate performance. On a macro level, the number of wins, goals for, and goals against were gross indicators of how they were doing. On a process level they had the clearly defined success factors mentioned earlier, reliably measured by a staff of regulars. Players were provided with feedback after each contest. Because the team was successful there was a positive climate and ample opportunity to acknowledge successful performance. Given these conditions, Team 1 players responded positively to feedback provided by the coaching staff.

Team 2 also had won-lost performance indicators. Unfortunately and overwhelmingly, that feedback highlighted their lack of success. They also had some event targets. However, process feedback was not as clearly defined or understood as Team 1's success factors. In addition, several players reported that failure to perform "the system" met with far less consequence with Team 2. One player said, "If I failed to make a play (when I was with Team 1), I would hear about it at the end of the shift. I might even miss a shift. Here, there isn't much consequence."

We have said that acknowledging success is an important part of the feedback process. Yet the climate on the losing team was charged with frustration and stress. While the coaching staff made a genuine effort to acknowledge positive performance, there was less opportunity to do so, and less of a climate to receive constructive criticism or praise.

Suggestions: Define, communicate, and explain meaningful success measures that match the talent and the mission. Provide consistent feedback and acknowledgement based on specific factors. Use more video training. Shaping should and could be used. Attach clear consequences to performing well (e.g., more play) or failing to perform the team's success factors (e.g., less play). Be encouraging. Be firm. Be consistent.

- **Confidence**

Confidence evolves out of both success and preparation. Team 1 was successful. They knew what was expected of them, prepared well, executed well . . . and approached each game with confidence, and the knowledge that they could compete successfully. They expected to win. It was part of their identity.

In contrast, Team 2's consistent lack of success undermined their confidence. Players were insecure. One player who came from the first-place to the last-place team said, "Here, you really can't trust the next guy to do his job. And," he added, "what really surprised me was after we lost, instead of getting pissed off, here they just accept it." Another player said of his Team 2 experience, "As disappointing as it may sound, we expected to lose. If we had a lead and the other team started to come back, the thought was, 'Here it goes again.'" What positive focus the players did have was more personal than team-oriented. Because of their lack of success and the lack of core leadership, members invested less in practicing and playing the team game. Consequently, they were less prepared, had less of the mindset that they would win . . . and were less confident.

John Wooden, one of basketball's most respected and successful coaches, has said of confidence, "The strongest steel is a well-founded self-belief. It is earned, not given."[2] Team 1 had it. Team 2 did not.

Suggestions: Remind Team 2's players of their long-term personal development goals. Simplify immediate team expectation, define clear directives, see that everyone understands, be encouraging, be demanding, attach consequence to performance, and build from mini accomplishable objectives (including achievable practice challenges) to more demanding goals.

- **Chemistry**

Chemistry relates to the social climate and the flow of positive energy, respect, and support that exists between team members.

Rob, a 10-year NHL veteran who played on several teams that were Stanley Cup contenders, related his belief that team chemistry was a key to the success of these competitive teams. When I asked him what contributed to the chemistry, he said, first it was management selecting people of character—players with talent, a positive work ethic, and a solid team attitude. Second, Rob (now a coach himself) described the motivation and ability of the coach to enroll all the players (veterans, rookies, stars, and fringe players), and to treat them all fairly. Third was the role of the team's core leaders, who saw to it that all players were included in team activities. "There were no cliques on these winning teams. We all got along."[3] The comparison of Teams 1 and 2, below, is consistent with Rob's observations.

Team 1 had good chemistry. Players consistently supported positive efforts in practice and in games. There were a number of contributing factors to Team 1's good chemistry. For starters, Team 1 selected players of good character (i.e., positive-minded, hard-working, team-oriented individuals). Second, a considerable effort was made to grow a positive team culture with team-building processes, leadership groups, one-on-one coaching, and sport psychology counseling. It should also be noted that it is easier to encourage, acknowledge, and support teammates in a winning environment.

On Team 2 there was a weak sense of team. Players stood up for each other in games and several of the players I interviewed described the Team 2 atmosphere as friendly. However, with little team building, weak core leadership, the team's losing record, and team residences spread out over a large urban area, there was little interaction away from the arena. Cliques were evident. One visual indicator of the team's weak chemistry could be seen at a team meal following a rare road victory. While most of the team ate together at one large table, veteran team leaders ate separately at another table in another section of the restaurant.

Suggestions: Acquire character individuals with leadership potential. Create success opportunities. Define clear, attainable performance goals and acknowledge positive improvement. Build relationships. Initiate team-building processes and leadership training, and integrate residences so that players are inclined to spend more time together "away from work."

- **Identity**

Team identity is a construct that speaks to who we are as an organization or group. Team 1 had a clear sense of being a smart, hard-working group of men who loved to compete and win. They knew what they had to do to be successful. They also spoke of being a group with supportive, loyal "functional family" values. Their identity was consistent with their coaching and their achievement.

One example of a Team 1 team-building process occurred following a retreat in which team history, values, and expectations were reviewed. The exercise consisted of the core leadership group discussing and defining (with the coaching staff present) "who we are as a team." The identity statement arrived at by the core group was then presented to the whole group in a poster format citing the team's values . . . which all the players signed. Team 1 players also participated in individual "coaching" sessions that addressed their role and contribution to the team's success.

Team 2 seemed like a collection of individuals. As mentioned, there were some cliques. There was little or no team-building. There was no mission statement or statement as to who they were as a group (other than an informal, "not very good"). Despite coaching efforts, player focus was primarily on individual effort and individual results.

A phenomenon I've frequently observed in sport, when a winning team member is being interviewed after a successful performance, is that he or she attributes most or all of that success to the team as a whole. The standard cliché is "I couldn't have done it without the rest of the guys." In contrast, when a team is losing, there is a tendency to disengage from the group, and in the same interview (especially following another loss) a typical response is "Well, I'm doing *my* job." These and similar comments could be observed in regard to Teams 1 and 2 respectively.

Comparing Teams 1 and 2 underscores the relevance of the nine keys to team success. These nine key characteristics can be used to better understand organizational success in any field.

In many ways successful corporations act like winning teams but on a much larger scale.

Using the nine keys let's take a brief look at the character of the Toyota Motor Corporation, one of the most successful "teams" in the automotive industry—a company that both Microsoft's Bill Gates and General Electric's Jack Welch have described as exemplary.[4]

Toyota: A Winning Corporation

• **Meaningful purpose**

Toyota has a sense of purpose that supersedes short-term gain. Their philosophical mission, the foundation for all other principles, is generating value for the customer, the economy, and the society.

I discussed Toyota with Jeffery Liker, an engineering professor who has studied the company for decades and has written several excellent books about it. I asked him if there was a goal at Toyota of wanting to be the best. He replied, "That depends what you mean by being the best. When you say the best, that implies competition, and they certainly encourage that. For them being the best could be a variety of different things, like being better than last year." He continued, "One of the biggest things that helps them improve as a company is what they call *hoshin kanri* planning. *Hoshin* means direction, and *kanri* is the means to achieve direction. It is Toyota's annual goal-setting process. It goes from the president in Japan, to the VPs, to the general managers, ultimately down to the group leaders and team leaders of the work groups on the factory floor in every Toyota plant. Each supervisor-subordinate pair comes to agreement on the goals, and the plans for achieving the goals. Each level establishes and commits to a number of challenging *hoshin* each year."[5]

At Toyota everyone is challenged to be the best they can be. And that means meeting (even exceeding) targets they set for quality, efficiency, delivery, cost, and safety. Meeting these performance targets is the way to realizing Toyota's core goals, which are improving quality to the customer through the process of building efficient, high-quality automobiles, and in so doing contributing to a healthier society.

Regarding this last point, in his book *Inside the Mind of Toyota*, Satoshi Hino suggests the goal of Toyota is to contribute to society by manufacturing high quality automobiles. He writes that those new employees who enter the company because they like cars will eventually be influenced by Toyota's founding principle and become aware that producing quality automobiles is a means of achieving the corporation's real purpose of contributing to society. When I asked Liker if Hino's comment was truly the case, and if it applied to Toyota employees in North America as well as to those in Japan, he wholeheartedly agreed.[6]

Team Toyota employees are aligned in their efforts toward achieving a meaningful purpose defined by a three-pointed mission statement: 1. To contribute to the economic growth in the country in which it is located. 2. To contribute to the stability and well-being of team members. (employees, suppliers). 3. To contribute to the overall growth of Toyota by adding value for customers. And they strive to do this with a two-pillar approach based on a commitment to continuous improvement (*kaizen*) and a respect for people.

• Talent

There is a lot of talk at Toyota about the people factor. In their book *Toyota Talent*, Jeffery Liker and David Meier suggest that Toyota doesn't just produce cars; it produces people.[7]

For starters, Toyota is selective about hiring, considerably more selective than the competition. In setting up a new parts plant in Hebron, Kentucky, Toyota received 13,500 applicants for 275 jobs. In their selection process they ran the applicants through job fairs, interviews, background checks, drug tests, and physical exams before offering the finalists a job.[8] Liker said, "Toyota looks for people who are motivated, team-oriented problem-solvers; people who are passionate about being excellent and possess leadership skills. If someone has these qualities Toyota assumes they can train them in the technical skills."[9] As stated in Chapter 2, when it comes to recruiting talent, winning teams, like Toyota, prize attitude over skill.

Hirotaka Takeuchi, Emi Osono, and Norihiko Shimizu studied Toyota for six years, visiting eleven countries; participating in numerous meetings, interviews, and events; and analyzing many internal documents. Regarding Toyota's unique attitude toward the workforce, they have written, "What's different is that the company views employees not just as a pair of hands but as knowledge workers who accumulate *chie*—the wisdom of experience—on the company's front lines. Toyota therefore invests heavily in people and organizational capabilities, and it garners ideas from everyone and everywhere: the shop floor, the office, the field."

In comparing the talent of the two teams in the previous section, one of the players who had been traded from Team 2 to Team 1 remarked, "Here they select good players, not necessarily the top picks, but good players. And what's really impressive is their ability to develop these players and make both them and the team better." At Toyota, they begin by selecting superior talent, then immerse the talent in a positive, high-performance culture, and develop them with an intensive, comprehensive training program that makes both the talent and the organization better.

• Leadership

The head leads and the body follows. Humility, vision, efficiency, a strong work ethic, a true *kaizen* spirit and a respect for people characterize Toyota's leadership.

Toyota's top-down leaders are experienced veterans of the Toyota Way. At the most senior level, Toyota's managers rise through the hierarchy slowly. In 2006, Toyota's executive vice presidents were on average sixty-one years of age (past the traditional retirement age of fifty-five of Japanese companies).[10] Despite their age, they are visionary, long-term planners, and leaders in innovation. For example, well over a decade ago Toyota committed to building and marketing hybrid vehicles. Competitors like GM, who had hybrid technology in advanced research labs a decade earlier, chose not to invest in it because of the initial costs. Recently GM vice chairman Bob Lutz was quoted as saying "We made a bad decision. Being known as a technology laggard is not conducive to selling automobiles."[11] Toyota is currently on their fourth generation of hybrids while North American automakers are struggling to catch up.

Toyota leadership embraces and reflects *kaizen*; in so doing they set challenging targets, and demand and enforce the highest standards of quality and efficiency. As with most winning teams strong leadership is not limited to the top . . . it flows right through the organization from the VPs down to team leaders who manage small work groups on the factory floor. At every level, leadership challenges, inspires, and supports their charges in meeting their *hoshin* and being number one in efficiency and quality.

• Game Plan/Strategy

Winning isn't just about working hard, it's working smart. Toyota's strategy is a combination of four factors: 1) a socially conscious, long-term vision for the corporation, 2) a lean, highly-efficient system of production (TPS) with clearly defined targets, 3) their *kaizen* commitment to innovation and quality, and 4) a genuine respect for the workers and partners.

Toyota Production System manufacturing system enables the Japanese giant to make the planet's best automobiles at the lowest cost and to develop new products quickly." As stated, both Jack Welch and Bill Gates have singled out Toyota Management as winners and models. Talking to a group of industrialists in Japan, Welch began by saying, "First of all, you have to learn the terms of winning from management techniques of companies like Toyota"[12]

In discussing Team 1's strategy earlier in this chapter, I referred to their seven success factors and mentioned that these factors were clearly understood and measurable. Toyota's success factors are reflected in meeting their targets, their *hoshin kanri*. The *hoshin* provides the direction, and the *kanri* provides the detailed plan which all have been involved in creating. The Toyota strategy includes implementing well-defined standardized procedures to accomplish the targets—and everything is measured. On the factory floor performance is measured down to (a few) defects per million, and work team metrics are recorded and posted daily.

The game plan at Toyota is one of vision, decision, efficient execution, a commitment to quality, efficiency, improvement, and there are clearly defined targets and processes in place to ensure the plan is realized.

• **Commitment**

We have defined commitment as the willingness to do what's necessary to achieve one's goal. As stated, Toyota's implementation of *kaizen* involves enrolling employees at every level of the organization to be responsible to meet targets and strive for perfection. Their commitment to continuous improvement and their pursuit of excellence exists in regard to quality, efficiency, and safety, as well as meeting moral and environmental standards. At Toyota employees don't passively wait for mistakes to happen or defects to surface. Rather, they continuously look with active eyes for ways to improve systems and add value.

Another expression of commitment (discussed in Chapter 5) is that in winning teams the "we" is greater than the "me." As discussed under "Talent" above, Toyota actively supports and coaches their "players" in becoming valuable, competent, permanent members of the Toyota family. In North America, many autoworkers see their first alliance not to the company but to their union. This is quite different from the situation at Toyota, where there are no unions and the ethic is one team and *kaizen*. Liker describes Toyota systems as "servant leadership"[13] where leaders serve the work teams that do the value-added work. Leaders are expected to put their egos aside and give credit to the team when good things are accomplished.

- **Feedback**

"Assess and adjust" is the cornerstone of progress and change.

As mentioned, Toyota is all about striving to innovate, standardize, assess and improve. In their quest to perfect and innovate, they have built in a system driven by objective, measurable performance goals at every step and every level of the organization. Along with macro measures of profitability and market share, players at every level of the Toyota team are challenged to meet measurable targets in quality, efficiency, delivery, and safety that they previously agreed to.

Regarding quality, as mentioned, every plant is challenged to produce a vehicle that is rated number one or two in quality in the JD Power survey. That challenge is scaled down through plant management to the factory floor and to each work team. Daily metrics record progress. These results are clearly posted. Employees know, often on a shift basis, where they are in regard to meeting their targets.[14]

Precise, regular feedback is very much part of the Toyota Way. At Toyota they define measurable targets, execute highly efficient standardized procedures, and track performance on a regular, daily basis.

- **Confidence**

Confidence evolves out of success and preparation. Toyota's lean and mean (TPS) production system, their *kaizen* attitude, their respect for people (the worker, supplier, and customer), and their intensive training have all contributed to their becoming the world's number one automaker.

Despite the rapid growth and remarkable success, Toyota employees don't exude excessive confidence. At Toyota, a strong push for continuous improvement, coupled with a sense of humility and the belief that we can always do better guards against over-confidence. A similar attitude is reflected in Tiger Woods commenting, "I can always do better."[15]

Jeffery Liker described Toyota employees as having a balance between a success mentality, a challenge mentality, and a humbleness mentality. He said, "The standard statement that you hear from the top is that complacency is our biggest enemy. There is always concern that someone is thinking we're perfect or we're the best. They want employees to feel there's a considerable gap between where we are and our goals. If you were to go to any manager in Toyota and ask 'Are you perfect?' the answer would be predictable. They would laugh and say, 'We have so far to go.

We're just really learning in America, and they are so far ahead of us in Japan.' Then, if you were to ask, 'Well, if I was to walk into a General Motors plant, compared to your plant where do you think the General Motors plant would be?' They would laugh and say somewhat cautiously, GM still has some work to do."[16]

There is a belief within the organization that pressure produces excellence. And both the pressure and the excellence are there. In terms of quality, and according to a Consumer Reports study, fifteen of the top thirty-eight most reliable models from any car manufacturer (over the previous seven-year period) were manufactured by Toyota/Lexus. In contrast, GM, Mercedes, and BMW had no cars on this list. Further, not a single Toyota vehicle was on Consumer Reports' dreaded "vehicles to avoid" list, while a number of Ford, GM, and Chrysler models were on the list. Another quality indicator reported by the Automotive Lease Guide found that after three years Toyota's models retain 52 percent of their value versus 43 percent for GM. They go on to conclude that's one reason why the Toyota Camry has been America's favorite car for the past five years, outselling GM's number one car, the Chevy Impala, by 35 percent in 2006.[17]

Even in challenging times Toyota appears relatively well positioned to adapt and carry on. Their systems are lean, efficient, and innovative; their plants are modern; workers are well-trained; and the corporation is well capitalized.

Contrast Toyota's situation and it's understandable that many of North America's big three automotive executives, plant operatives, and shareholders are less than confident about the immediate future.

• Chemistry

Toyota is family. There are no unions and no appreciable labor–management strife.

At Toyota there is relative job security. The last decision management will make is to lay off full-time employees. During the economic downturn (experienced at the time of this writing), competitors closed numerous plants and announced thousands of layoffs. In contrast, Toyota, which halted production of trucks in two plants (in Indiana and Texas), kept approximately 4000 full-time workers on the payroll, essentially doing non-moneymaking things to develop their people (like training, or loaning them out to volunteer agencies in the area).[18]

As we said in Chapter 8, chemistry is about respect. At Toyota workers are respected if they perform. They are given every opportunity and encouragement to perform, and they are challenged. Teruyuki Minouri, a Toyota Senior Managing Director has said, "There can be no success making things (*monozukuri*) without making people (*hitozukuri*)." Referring to Toyota's production system he said, "An environment where people have to think brings with it wisdom and wisdom brings with it *kaizen* (continuous improvement). It is a basic characteristic of human beings that they develop wisdom from being put under pressure. Perhaps the greatest strength of the Toyota Production System is the way it develops people."[19]

Good chemistry is also characterized by flow. At Toyota, team play is emphasized and decisions are made by consensus. And product flows through and between units. Workers compete to meet targets, to exceed last year's numbers, and to outperform departments in plants making similar models. However, there is no intra-plant competition between work teams, which could disrupt chemistry.

It's the same in sport. As Pat Riley has said:

For a team made up of highly specialized players, the worst way to compare performance is between each other. The best

basis is versus the players on competing teams or against
his own history.
—Pat Riley, *The Winner Within: A Life Plan for Team Players*[20]

Healthy people want to excel. At Toyota work is paced and permanent, absenteeism is very low, and employees feel a sense of participation in increasing their company's market share worldwide. All that contributes to good chemistry.

- **Identity**

Our identity affects how we perform and how others react to us. Team members of many successful organizations project a kind of self-assurance and sense of pride. I asked Jeffery Liker if there was a special sense amongst Toyota employees that they are part of an extraordinary organization. He answered that along with a sense of humility and a belief that we can do better, there is also a sense that we are good.

Perhaps the greatest indicator of a positive identity and a positive feeling for Toyota is that people want to work there. Jeffery Liker said, "Toyota is an exemplary organization and a lot of companies try to imitate Toyota. If you work for Toyota that's a great credential. Toyota doesn't pay particularly well, especially as you go up the ranks. At the management and executive levels Toyota pays a percentage, maybe half of what other companies are paying for people that level." He continued, "In the last few years, anybody at the manager, general manager level or above, could double their salary simply by leaving Toyota and making a phone call. And yet they don't. There is very little turnover at Toyota, only about three percent per year." Further, Toyota's CEO is paid approximately one-tenth of what the CEOs of Ford and GM take home. Liker concluded, "Certainly some people leave Toyota for what they think are greener pastures, but there are a whole lot of people there who don't want to leave Toyota, who think it's a great company. And in spite of the fact they could make considerably more money elsewhere, they won't leave."[21]

It's not often in professional sport that we see a star athlete stay with a team when he could have been paid twice as much elsewhere. When people are consistently willing to sacrifice salary to be part of the team, it's usually an indication that the team they are willing to play for is a very special team. That's Toyota.

Bottom line: Toyota's image, within and without, is that of a successful, innovative organization, providing the public with superior product quality, reliability and value—and a good company to work for . . . a company with character.

EVALUATE:

Take some time to sit back, and using the nine keys as a guide, reflect on the team(s) of which you are currently a part. Acknowledge those qualities that are team strengths that you want to reinforce and consider those qualities or keys that could be enhanced to provide you and your teammates with greater success and well-being. (See Exercise 1 in Chapter 12).

CHAPTER 11

DIFFERENT TEAMS, DIFFERENT DEMANDS

Teamwork is neither "good" nor "desirable." It is a fact.
Wherever people work together or play together they do so as a
team. Which team to use for what purpose is a crucial, difficult
and risky decision that is even harder to unmake. Managements
have yet to learn how to make it.
—Peter Drucker, professor of management, author

Some coaching elements, like those that promote focus, effort, and chemistry, facilitate success in all team situations. However, the unique challenges characterized by different sports (e.g., baseball, football) and different business functions (e.g., sales, manufacturing) require a somewhat different coaching emphasis in order to maximize team success. For example, when consulting with a baseball team or a sales team, I work more with team members on their individual expression of ability. When consulting with a basketball or hockey team, or a marketing or management group, I am more concerned with helping individuals synergize their skill sets with those of their team mates.

Different Sports, Different Business Processes/Different Coaching

To maximize success, some sports and some business functions emphasize the plan; others emphasize the flow between team members; and others emphasize the individual.

The Game of the Plan

Football is a game of the plan, where authority flows vertically and top down. In football, a small group of individuals, the coaching staff, confer and create a game plan, which they then pass down to the team. (Remember the Monday morning meeting example.) Preparation is key. Indeed, a point that coaches Shula and Parcells made earlier is that in games of the plan preparation is vital to team success.

All week long football teams practice executing the plan. Then, on game day, they are challenged to perform according to plan. Operating the plan efficiently, controlling the ball, and not allowing any turnovers or fumbles, produces a win.

As Robert Keidel noted in his book *Game Plans: Sport Strategies for Business*[1] that is the model of the factory and manufacturing. In manufacturing, a small group of individuals (the executive group or the board) determines what's to be produced and how it's to be done. They raise capital, build the plant, and install and staff the assembly line. Successful operation of the assembly line is similar to successful implementation of the game plan. Like football, the workers are utilized as replaceable parts. They are trained to perform specific functions, do them well, on line, and on time. If one part isn't functioning it is replaced and the assembly line keeps running. Success in the factory, profitability, is keeping the assembly line running smoothly no turnovers, no fumbles.

While there's a time and place to communicate a good idea (e.g., quality circles), individual creativity and freelancing "on line" is no more the order of the day than making up plays in a football huddle. Success is a product of working the plan. The plan is supreme.

On the football field or the factory floor what defines the bottom line is that winning teams are organized groups, directed from above, with a clear understanding or roles and responsibilities, successfully executing the plan.

The Flow Game

Hockey, basketball, and soccer are different. They are horizontal, flow games. For a hockey, basketball, or soccer team to be successful they have to play together, flow together, passing the ball or puck. Moving it A to B to A to C to D to A . . . is flow. The synergy that comes from passing the ball/puck around, and back and forth, generates scoring opportunities. Working together and using each other effectively is a key to success.

Roger Neilson, a famous and innovative hockey coach, related an experience of lining his players up on the blue line at practice and telling each "line" (i.e., trio of skaters) to skate as fast as they could to the far end of the rink. When he blew the whistle, the first line sprinted down the ice as fast as they could. When they were about halfway to the far end of the rink, Roger fired a puck at the end boards. The puck beat the players to the end boards. Then he blew the whistle again and the second line took off at full speed. Again, he waited until they were half way there and fired the puck, which beat the players to the end boards. The same thing was repeated with the third and fourth line. Always, the puck got there first. Eventually one of the players asked, "Rog, what's the point? The puck's always going to get there first."

"Exactly," replied Neilson. "The puck travels faster than you can skate. If you want to win, pass the puck."[2]

Success in hockey, basketball, and soccer is about flowing together, moving, passing, generating scoring chances. In these sports, teams win when people play together, flow together . . . and the synergy of their efforts and interactions creates scoring opportunities and makes things happen.

In business, that's the model of marketing or brainstorming (e.g., product development). In marketing you have a group of individuals working together, passing ideas back and forth. The synergy of their interaction produces new business ideas, possibilities, and plans. Unlike football and manufacturing, this is a horizontal as opposed to vertical process, and successful coaching must take that into account.

I was consulting with Corona, a company that manufactures superior-quality garden tools. The president of the company, a former member of the NASA team, ran the plant and the forge with a controlled, lean, "just in time" exactness. One day he asked me to facilitate a brainstorming session on new product possibilities. To support the creative process a characteristic of such sessions is that participants put judgment aside and share a variety of innovative and sometimes bizarre product suggestions and ideas. However, in this instance, rather than letting their creativity roll, the president responded to each idea he didn't like with instant critical feedback. Not surprisingly, the group stopped offering up ideas.

During a break in the meeting, I quietly explained to the president that he was a football coach (and a very good one). He was very effective at overseeing the team operating according to plan. However, the brainstorming game we were playing in the room was basketball. It was a horizontal, flow game of moving ideas (the ball) around in an effort to come up with a unique, creative scoring opportunity. When the president understood that his controlling, vertical football style of leadership, so appropriate to the manufacturing process, was actually suppressing the group's creativity and flow, he withdrew expressing judgment, and the synergy re-emerged.

Leadership can be somewhat directive in coaching flow, but too much vertical input limits horizontal energy and team synergy.

The "I" Game

Baseball is an "I" game. It's an individual–team sport. The pitcher on the mound or the batter at the plate may wear the uniform of the Yankees, the Dodgers, or the Blue Jays, but they are essentially individual operators, relying on their personal resources to compete successfully. Of course, there is a wonderful flow of energy between the shortstop, second and first basemen in executing the double play. However, baseball is more of an "I" game with the pitcher on the mound and the batter at the plate, performing solo, in turn.

From a coaching perspective, the key to winning in baseball is selecting the right players, building their confidence, and placing them in situations where they can perform and excel.

One World Series winning manager described his role very well. "As manager, the question is, how do you use your players? My job is to give the player the opportunity to be successful, whether the job is big or small. You want to put a player in a situation where he can do really well, to give him a chance to contribute or win, to make a star out of him. Then you have one less guy to worry about. Don't put him in situations he can't handle and where he won't shine. What good is that?" He continued, "I took a player who couldn't cut it as a starter and I made him a long relief pitcher. In this role he came into the game when the starter couldn't hold it. The situation gave him a chance to win the game. I knew he could do it. With success his confidence grew. He began to feel good about himself and he performed accordingly. He was no longer one of the maligned players; he was someone who contributed, someone who makes a difference."[3]

Managing baseball is putting the right player in the right situation and then building on his success. And with their success, baseball players are paid significant incentives based on individual (not team) performance. If and when they are traded to another team, a baseball player simply changes uniforms, taking his contracts, incentives, and batting averages with him to his new team. Baseball is an "I" game.

That's the model of sales. As mentioned earlier, being the member of a sales team is an individual challenge. Managing a successful sales team is about selecting the right individuals, sharpening their skill sets, building their confidence and their belief that they can . . . and then putting them in situations where they can perform.

I discussed the parallel between baseball and sales with DL, the vice president of financial services for a large credit union. He agreed. His comment was, "Managing a team of highly paid, independent, and entrepreneurial sales people in the financial services industry is a challenge. The team is really a collection of individuals working quite independently under a single banner. Each member of the team effectively runs his or her own small business. And, like a sports team, each of our 'players' has strengths and weaknesses. The trick to managing the team effectively is understanding the strengths each member possesses, helping them to stay motivated and focused, and moving them towards, and supporting them in, situations where they—and ultimately the team—will be successful."

Different Stages

Winning is the right leader leading the right people, at the right time.

We have described leadership and talent as keys to team success. One subject that hasn't been addressed is timing. Just as the different kinds of business and sport challenges demand different coaching emphases for success, individuals and teams at different stages of development require a different emphasis or style of leadership to be maximally effective.

A fundamental biological principle is that ontogeny recapitulates phylogeny. It means that in the development of the individual we can trace the development of the species. Similarly, the development of the individual parallels the development of the organization. In general, people and teams go through a similar maturation process. And, like people, teams in their early and more formative stages need strong clear direction and support. As a team develops or evolves, players may be given more freedom and autonomy to exercise their power and judgment in leading themselves.

Bruce Tuckman's team development model provides a helpful explanation of how teams develop and suggests the leadership appropriate at each stage. The model includes four basic stages that Tuckman refers to as forming, storming, norming, and performing.[4]

First is a *forming* stage, where the team members come together. At this stage there is a high dependence on the leader for direction and guidance. Individual roles and responsibilities are unclear. The leader, very much in charge, defines the team's purpose, objectives, and processes. Strong, directive, leadership is required.

Next is a *storming* stage, where there may be power struggles as teammates vie for position. At this stage, there is greater clarity of purpose than in the forming stage, but plenty of uncertainty still exists. A storming team needs to stay focused on its goals and avoid becoming distracted by relationship and emotional issues. Strong direction and control is required.

A good example of the successful evolution of a team through the storming phase and on into the norming and performing stages was Team USA's "Miracle on Ice" hockey gold medal victory at the 1980 Olympic Games. The collection of individuals that initially formed the team brought their personal histories and past rivalries and resentments to training camp. Early on, egos clashed and the storming expressed itself in open confrontation. With strong, top down leadership what emerged was a selfless group of dedicated team players focused on a collective goal that all bought into and performed very well.

Storming is followed by a *norming* stage, where there is growing agreement and consensus among the group. The leader now provides more facilitation than authoritarian direction. Team roles and responsibilities are understood and accepted, and major decisions are made with group agreement. Commitment and unity are growing. Some leadership is now shared with the group.

Last, there is a *performing* stage, where the team has considerable autonomy. The focus is about achieving goals. Team members make decisions utilizing criteria agreed upon with the leader. If and when disagreements occur they tend to be resolved within the team. Many changes to team process are also made by and within the team. The leader simply delegates and oversees.

Clearly, different styles of leadership are required for different stages of development. As the team evolves and matures, the authority and freedom extended by the leader to the team increases, while the leader's control and direction diminishes.

Chris played on a team of "all stars" that won two consecutive world championships. The coach of the team had the reputation of being a tough, no-nonsense, authoritarian leader. When I asked Chris what is was like to play under his "my way or the highway" style of leadership, he replied, "It worked very well for the short time (three weeks) we were together. We had a bunch of young guys from all over the country with considerable talent and sizable egos. And we had [a] really short time to form as a team and then to compete and win. So it was pretty intense and the way he approached it worked well."

Then he added, "But I don't know if I'd enjoy or thrive playing under that intense style of leadership over the long haul."

Individually and collectively, winning is a growth process. And growth must be nurtured and supervised. I have worked with "captain's groups" in both sport and industry. These are meetings of emerging team-leaders in which we discuss and coach team members on how to take more of a leadership role within the team.

Leadership is a learning process and the captains' group is a learning space. It's an opportunity to learn about how and when to lead. Most of the captain's groups I've worked with comprise six to eight individuals and meet every month or two. In these meetings we discuss visioning. Visioning involves exploring the team's goals and visualizing the end result the team is working towards. We discuss the behaviors and actions required by team leaders and the rank and file to produce that end result. We discuss what this group of leaders can do to facilitate that happening. We consider the kind and style of communication that would motivate and encourage individual and team performance. We consider ways to support positive performance and ways to deal with underachieving or inappropriate teammates. And we underline the importance of team leaders modeling the behaviors they want others to implement.

Periodically, we ask that elite group to provide each other with candid feedback as to how they are performing, and what the team needs more of from each of them. (See the leader in "The Person in the Middle" in Exercise 2, Chapter 12). One team I worked with had a strong, vocal captain who did everything he could to inspire his teammates, give them feedback, and organize team activities. He was a very positive model—and a dominating one. The challenge of the captain's group was to help the captain–leader to delegate more, and to allow and encourage his assistants to exercise their response-ability and power to become a stronger, more positive voice. Feedback involved giving the emerging leaders examples of when and how to express direction and reinforcement, and highlighting the importance of modeling.

A corporate middle management team also had a tendency to wait for their leader, the CFO, to tell them what to do. A process we focused on in the captain's group involved getting the participants to exercise more initiative in visioning how things should be run, and defining personal and team ABC's. In both group and individual coaching sessions the captains were also encouraged to more assertively communicate direction and feedback (to their staff), and model the initiative and drive a team needs to evolve, and to realize its goals and potential.

Captain's groups can be effective at improving leadership at all levels of an organization. The supervisor of a blue-collar warehouse crew created a captain's group in support of the team's goal to boost performance and be "best in class." The supervisor defined the purpose of the captain's group to the crews as follows: 1. To discuss what's working and what's not working on the shift, and what's required to raise the level of performance. 2. To determine who needs help to improve their performance and who can coach them best. 3. To identify who's performing exceptionally well and decide how best to recognize them. 4. To determine what's needed to raise the spirit of the team, and how and when to recognize team milestones. 5. To come up with ways to reinforce the team's performance ABCs. 6. To decide on ways to deal with employees who aren't performing up to the level of the team's expectations.

The supervisor also explained that she wanted the group to consider practical solutions to three issues: How do we take our performance to the next level? How do we recognize extraordinary performance? And how do we make the dream of being "best in class" motivating and relevant?

One of the concerns that the supervisor had regarding establishing a captain's group was how people in this union shop would react to the selection process. She wondered if it might not be seen as a special, elite group, and if there might not be some upset from people who were excluded from the group (that is, wanting in but not being selected).

I explained, "We want people to want to be a part of the captain's group. It is a group of better performers, people with leadership qualities who are positive models. We want people to want to take a leadership role in improving performance and creating a more effective team." When I followed up with the warehouse senior manager two months after my coaching session, he reported that the captain's group was a success. People wanted to be part of it, and the group was tackling relevant, team performance issues.

In discussing leadership earlier, I referred to a conversation with Gord Huston, the CEO of Envision Financial, a very successful credit union in the Pacific northwest, who said his job was to find good people interested in moving the organization forward and to develop these people. He said, "It's as though many people have a gremlin inside of them that's saying 'Don't make a mistake,' or 'Don't fail.' My job is to figure out a way to transform that inner voice and help them unleash their real potential. Ultimately, it's to encourage and empower them to run this organization well."[5]

The overwhelming majority of us live, work, and perform in teams. It is important that we learn to *use* our team experiences as a way to evolve into being better players and leaders, as well as healthier, happier individuals.

EVALUATE:

What type of game plan best fits the style of your team's operation?

Do you see the team experience as more of a plan, flow, or "I" game?

Do you feel leadership is taking the right approach, playing the right game?

How do you fit into this game plan?

The developmental stage also impacts on leadership style. Where on the developmental continuum does your team fit? Is it forming, storming, norming, or performing?

What do you think you can do personally to help bring your team to the next stage?

What can be done to move the team along the developmental continuum?

CHAPTER 12

APPLICATIONS
AND TEAM EXERCISES

Build for your team a feeling of oneness, of dependence on one another
and of strength to be derived by unity.
—Vince Lombardi

Coming together is a beginning. Keeping together is progress.
Working together is success.
—Henry Ford

A variety of group activities fall under the rubric of team-building. Essentially there are three kinds of activities.

1. The most basic team-building exercises are recreational in nature. Activities like golf, skiing, bowling, rafting, cruising, picnics, movies, casino nights, and a variety of assorted outings are designed to bring people together to bond outside the standard work environment. It is presumed this recreational interaction improves team chemistry and culture, and ultimately leads to better performance. Things can be done to enhance interaction in these activities. For example, in golfing outings, scramble and best ball formats allow co-workers to play together in teams, interacting and contributing in a positive, enjoyable manner.

2. Another variety of team-building is more problem-solving in nature. These activities involve giving the group a task (unrelated to the team's regular job) and having them work together to solve it. Presumably, participants learn something of how they and others interact around the challenge and also come to appreciate their fellow team members in a new light for their ingenuity, personality, and skill. Examples of some problem-solving activities I've used include imaginary survival scenarios (e.g., if a plane crashes in the jungle or desert, what do we as a group have to do to survive), creative scavenger hunts, physical cooperative activities like team relays (where the team has to stay together as they compete, rope climb, or build a boat from planks, rope, and tires, and then paddle it across a pond). These activities should be entertaining as well as challenging. Not only can they draw the group together, they often bring out leadership and character features from team members (some may not possess leadership roles in the day-to-day team environment) and generally improve players' understanding and appreciation of each other.

3. A third type of team-building activity includes those that develop awareness (either personal or organizational awareness) and relate somewhat more directly to the work the team does. It is this latter group of team insight exercises that I want to address.

Nine Team Insight Exercises

1. **Team Reflection–Action:** A team-building exercise that I have found useful is to review the nine keys to winning with an entire team, and then ask members to evaluate their team on a five-point scale in regard to each of these elements (1= completely

unsatisfactory; 5 = excellent). The group can caucus and choose one or two elements to work to improve in the next quarter or six months, and then prepare a plan of action to achieve that result.

I spoke to approximately a hundred managers and supervisors of a successful public transit company. After an hour-long seminar during which we discussed these nine keys, the group was asked to evaluate their organization in regard to each element. An electronic system was used that provided instantaneous and anonymous feedback. Once we had an overview of the team members' perception of how their organization stacked up on the nine keys, the various specialized organizational sub-teams (e.g., finance, operations, security) met together separately, caucused opinion, and decided which of the nine elements their specific sub-team was going to address and work to improve during the next six-month period. Each group then related their decision to the entire organizational gathering, along with why they chose that particular element, as well as how improving performance in that area could improve both their unit's performance and performance of the entire corporation. Thereafter, the CEO asked each group to have a plan of action for their proposed improvement on his desk within two weeks.

When I followed up with the CEO two months after the exercise, he reported that all action plans came in on time. He felt that implementing the program would make his organization a better team. What's more, he felt the whole exercise raised awareness of relevant team process issues and brought the people within the organization closer together.

Similarly, I have reviewed the nine keys with a number of corporate and sport teams. While the business groups involved have been quite variable in size from six to 150 people, the sport teams usually consisted of twenty to thirty members, including players and coaches. After reviewing the nine keys, we discuss which ones the team needs to focus on to improve performance. A plan of action follows, along with a commitment to improve performance in the selected areas.

A variation of this approach that I've participated in successfully is to consider a business case study or view a video/film of a winning (or losing) sport team and then analyze and discuss the success or failure of the organization, using the nine keys to stimulate thought and discussion.

2. **What We Appreciate and What We Need More Of:** This team-building exercise is an opportunity for collective peer feedback, and is similar to the 360-degree exercise discussed in Chapter 5, though much quicker to implement and more peer-based. It can be carried out in several different ways:

    • **The Person in the Middle**
    The team assembles. Essentially, one member takes a seat in the center surrounded by his or her peers. One after another, team members share their perception and provide feedback regarding how the team member in the center impacts on the team. They share both the person in the center's strengths; specifically, what the person in the middle contributes to the success of the team, and, also what he or she could improve upon, or what the team needs more of from this person. Doing the Person in the Middle exercise with an entire team of twenty people, as described above, can be a lengthy process.

    • **Shorter Variation**
    A time-saving variation of the feedback exercise incorporating the whole team involves pairing up group members. Then,

one member of each pair is asked to comment about his or her partner's strengths, something positive the person brings to the team, and something the team needs more of from this person. When they have finished, the other member of the pair does the same. This process is carried out for all pairs (one pair at a time) in front of the entire team.

Not surprisingly, there is a tendency, particularly in this format, for team members to be excessively generous about their partner's positive contribution to the team. Often what is more cogent and useful is the feedback about what the team needs more of from the person in question.

- **Team-Leader Variation**

A leadership variation of the Person in the Middle is doing the exercise with just five or six team leaders, as opposed to doing it with the whole team. I have done this with as many as eight leaders. I found it helpful to have each of the leaders write down what each of their co-leaders brings to the team, both positively, and also what the team needs more of from them. Then I collect, shuffle, and redistribute the papers and have each leader read from the sheet they were given what was said about the person in the middle, first acknowledging them positively for their contribution to the team . . . and then suggesting what the team needs more of from them.

For the Person in the Middle exercise to be effective, perspective and maturity are required. For maximal impact, and to avoid conflict, it is important to have a clear understanding that the focus of the exercise is to improve team performance and that a positive, supportive, respectful context provides an optimal opportunity for meaningful communication. Feedback on areas to improve, or things that the team needs more of from the person in the middle, should be seen as honest feedback from mature, caring colleagues.

If a team member's commitment is to be the best he or she can be, the person should welcome the feedback and use it to be a more effective performer and to move the team forward. The only response to the group's feedback encouraged and required by the person in the middle is a simple "thank you."

I have conducted this exercise in all three formats a number of times with a variety of sport and business groups. It has always been useful.

3. **The Logo Exercise:** Who are we? What do we want to become?

In these times of branding consciousness, the logo exercise can be both motivating and perspective-enhancing. First, project the logo of a well-known and highly successful sport team or corporation. Next ask the group what that logo means to them, what feelings and impressions it brings to mind. In business, that could be the logo of Microsoft, Shell, Mercedes, Google, or Toyota. In sport that could be the logo of the New England Patriots, New York Yankees or Giants, Boston Red Sox, or the Detroit Red Wings.

In response to the question, "What does this logo mean to you?" people frequently reply with comments like "Winners, unity of purpose, good leadership, hard work, good team chemistry, determination, perseverance, star players, big salaries."

Next, I project their team's logo onto the screen, and ask the group what they want their logo to represent this year, in a year or two, or in the next five years. The logo is a symbol of the identity of the group. To team members it represents who they are or what they are becoming. And that symbol can energize. I continue the process by asking the group what has to happen in the way of focus, effort, and commitment to make that image of success a reality.

For contrast, I have also projected the logo of a company or team with a notoriety for failure, or even the logo of a group that went up like a Roman candle, and then after a brief flash of fame came crashing down. I then ask the group for input on what that logo represents, as well as the possible perceived causes for failure.

As a sequel I often end the exercise by projecting a cartoon on the screen. It's the cartoon of a group of six geese walking along looking up at the sky where high above them a V of geese is flying. One of the geese on the ground is looking up and saying, "Hey, look what they're doing."[1] I ask the audience, "Who do you identify with? Who do you want to be? Is it the high flyers—the trend-setters doing something extraordinary? Or do you see yourself as one of those other critters shuffling along on the ground admiring the accomplishments of others? The choice is yours. Your thoughts and your efforts create your reality."

4. **Overcoming Inertia: The Power of All:** In writing my book *Hockey Tough: A Winning Mental Game*,[2] I talked with Joe Thornton, an NHL all-star and former captain, about leadership. Joe said, "A team is like a locomotive. To get it rolling everybody has to work together and everybody has to play a role. Once it gets going, then it can become a powerful force."

A simple, physical exercise to graphically illustrate the power of people working together involves asking individual team members to push or pull a large bus in order to get it moving. Hard as they may try, it is not possible for one, or even a couple of the team's "stars" or leaders, to overcome inertia and get the bus moving. However, when all the team are contributing, pushing or pulling together, the bus gradually begins to move and once it gets rolling with everyone's help, it moves along relatively easily.

What is also worth illustrating is that while it takes considerable energy and everyone working together to get things rolling, once they're rolling, a few people offering resistance can slow the momentum and even bring the bus to a halt.

The point of the exercise is readily experienced. We must all work together to get things moving and continue to work together to realize our goal. This exercise is particularly well-suited to sport teams who express themselves physically and who frequently travel on a team bus.

5. **Leadership for All:** Leadership is a vital component to team success. In Chapter 3 I discussed both top down leadership and leadership provided by the rank and file. As mentioned, to enhance team leadership I frequently establish leadership or "captain's groups" to coach people how to lead more effectively. We look at visioning, leadership opportunities, communication, and reinforcement. Of course team success isn't just about the mindset of a select few. Every team member makes a difference. With that thought in mind, a simple team-building process I recommend involves going over some of the components that enhance leadership with the entire team in order to help everyone become a better team player. The exercise involves having people read and discuss the following elements (adapted from *The Team Captain's Leadership Manual*[3]) and then consider situations where they can apply (and could have applied) these qualities to their daily performance.

- Commitment

  I am one of the hardest workers on the team.

  I care passionately about the team's success.

  I am a competitive person who wants to win/succeed every day.

- Confidence

  I believe in myself. I give my teammates confidence.

  I love to perform in a pressure situation. Under pressure I get stronger.

  I am a positive person. I bounce back quickly following mistakes and errors.

- Composure

  I stay composed in pressure situations.

  I stay positively focused when faced with adversity, obstacles, and distractions.

  I keep my anxiety, anger, and frustration under control.

- Feedback

  I regularly encourage my teammates to do their best.

  I am a player who seeks to unify the team and make us better.

  I communicate determination and optimism when the team is struggling.

  I constructively confront my teammates when necessary.

- Modeling

  Modeling is one of the most powerful forms of learning.

  I model success in my thoughts and actions.

  I make my teammates better.

6. **Team Identity:** I am often asked by coaches to help strengthen their group's identity as a winning team. One exercise I discussed in Chapter 9 and have found to be effective in growing a positive group identity involves exploring two concepts with the group:

Concept 1: Winning teams are like a healthy, functional family.

Concept 2: Winning teams love to win and know and do what it takes to succeed.

In exploring the qualities that characterize a *healthy, functional* family, one group I worked with described healthy family values this way:

Responsible: Family members understand the demands of the family and strive to meet the family's expectations.

Hard Working and Self-Sacrificing: Family members will sweat and sacrifice for the family good.

Respectful: Family members respect themselves and others, regardless of size, shape, role, or personality. They respect the golden rule of do onto others what you would have them do unto you.

Caring: A family cares for each other. Family members will do anything to help each other.

Supporting: Family members help other family members to do, be, and look their best.

Trusting: A solid family value is "you can count on me" in good times and bad. A family comes together in times of adversity.

Loyal: A family doesn't give up on family members.

Communicating: Family members communicate clearly and honestly with each other. They say it like it is. They listen, acknowledge, advise, and support.

In exploring the behavior of teams that love to win, and know how to win, one group said, "Teams that love to win work hard, work smart, work the system, and work together. They believe in themselves and each other." In regard to working smart and working the system, one team I worked with defined seven success factors that are the guidelines to their success in their sport. As I explained in Chapter 6, the team understood exactly what each success factor was and why each factor was important. Then it was up to them to perform and they did, winning the championship.

Knowing who you are, what has to be done, and why, respecting each person's role, and working together are the building blocks of a winning team identity.

In challenging times, when there are unusual stresses, or simply from time to time, it's good to go back to basics and remind the group that we are family and that we are a team that loves to win and knows and does what it takes to win. That's who we are.

• Burying the Past

Whenever I work with a team, I usually pick up something interesting and often useful.

I was called upon to consult with a sport team that was really struggling and its players were losing heart. They were not feeling good about their performance and teams around the league perceived them in a negative light. In an effort to turn things around, the coach held a meeting and asked the players to list the negative things they were thinking about the team, and what they believed others were saying about them. He had an assistant write their remarks on a large piece of paper. He then had the players accompany him outside where he took the paper filled with their remarks, poured lighter fluid on it, and set it aflame. Players watched it burn. The coach then asked the players to bury the ashes.

When they went back inside, the coach told the team. "We've buried the past. Now, let's create a new self-image." He placed another large piece of paper on the wall and asked the players to come up with a new positive mission statement for the team. He also said, "Based on our strengths and commitment let's redefine who we are as a team, and what we are committed to achieving." Their comments were recorded. It was an engaging exercise; players responded and it lifted the spirit of the team . . . temporarily. However, the increase was short-lived. Unless the ceremony of burying the past is supported with adequate talent, effective systems, and suitable preparation, any gains will be temporary at best.

"Burying the past" can be a useful exercise for short-circuiting a slump or drop in performance and the negative thinking that engenders. However, to have more than just a temporary effect, it's essential that the team in question possess the keys of talent, leadership, strategy, preparation, and commitment to support their "refreshed" identity.

7. **Personal Identity:** Successful team performance is based on individual team members having a strong sense of self and their role. Clarity builds confidence, and since we get more of what we think about, one exercise I have found to be helpful both

as a form of mental preparation and in building personal and organizational confidence (and one I describe in Chapter 9) is to think, "I am a good _____."

(Fill in the blank with whatever it is you do—e.g., player, manager, and then complete the following.)

When I perform at my best I:

_____

_____

_____

Fill in the blanks with six to eight specific actions that highlight you performing well and are clear enough that you can actually picture being or doing them.

Dan, a Microsoft veteran, completed the exercise for three of the different roles he plays in the organization.[4]

• **As a software developer:**

I am an outstanding software engineer.

I create high-quality software and ship it on time.

I architect my components ahead of time and refine my designs as I go.

I create simple, elegant designs.

I understand my customers and keep them in mind as I develop my software.

I periodically check in with them to gather their feedback on the software I've created.

I engage with the community that uses my software.

I work well with other engineers, both on my team and in partner teams.

I find defects as early in the development cycle as possible, minimizing the cost to correct them.

I learn from my mistakes, fix those issues in other code that already exists, and avoid them in writing new code.

I communicate my ideas well, verbally and in writing. I am able to effectively explain concepts to diverse audiences, including those that have technical expertise and those who do not.

My code is well-documented and easily maintainable.

- **As a salesman:**

I am an outstanding salesman.

I understand my customers, and address their needs as well as my own and the needs of my company.

I am ethical, honest, and forthright.

I meet and exceed my quotas/target numbers on a regular basis.

I proactively gather feedback from my customers, and work diligently to improve my customer satisfaction metrics.

I use my expertise and close relationship with customers to positively impact the future direction of my company's products/services.

I cultivate business and personal relationships with my existing customers, and network frequently in order to find new customers for my business.

I represent my company in the most positive and professional manner possible.

I exemplify my company's values.

- **As an executive:**

I make rational decisions in a timely manner.

I remove myself as a bottleneck in the process, and delegate authority where it makes sense to do so.

I balance both short-term and long-term perspectives.

I am able to empathize with others and understand their perspectives.

I listen to others before speaking.

I engage at the appropriate level of detail, depending on the particular topic, my own expertise, the forum, and audience.

I communicate clearly and effectively, both verbally and in writing.

I give strong presentations, taking my audience into account, projecting an aura of competency and confidence.

I make others better.

I leverage the individual strengths of members of my team, and enable them to spend most of their time doing what they do best.

I develop the members of my team, taking their career aspirations into account.

I make my team feel valued.

I create a productive, collaborative team environment.

I lead others with confidence and earned authority.

I earn the trust of my team, my peers, and my superiors.

I get things done effectively and efficiently.

I get things that need to get done now, and make strategic investments that allow me to get things done in the future.

Individually the exercise builds confidence and consistency. When an entire team prepares accordingly, there is a clear sense of roles and greater team consistency and confidence.

8. **Personal Power:** How we feel affects how we perform. It also affects team confidence and chemistry. One aide to managing emotions and feeling more confident and in control is learning how to breathe consciously. As mentioned in Chapter 7, conscious breathing connects mind and body. Anxious thinking is characterized by an excess of negative, worrisome thoughts of the past or the future, and about things over which we have little or no control. Focusing on breathing brings one back to the

present . . . where the power is. Whatever the challenge, it is best dealt with in the present. As you tune into your breathing, the thought is, "There is only this breath." Taking a few minutes to focus on breathing (especially on drawing in energy with each inhalation) brings a renewed energy, competence, and calm back to the breather, all of which builds confidence.

As described, I coach my clients to cue three things in the breathing.

1. The first is rhythm. That means feeling or experiencing the breath flowing in and feeling or experiencing the breath flowing out.

   The breath is like waves in the ocean. Continuously flowing in and out.

   To feel more confident and powerful, I encourage clients to take the time (even if it's only five minutes a day) to experience their natural breathing rhythm. There is power in rhythm.

2. The second breathing cue involves bringing more awareness to the in-breath. I remind my clients that if breathing is respiration, then the in-breath is the inspiration. To inspire yourself, be conscious of drawing energy in with each in-breath. "You have a personal connection to an unlimited supply. Draw energy to you."

3. The third breathing focus is direction. It is about directing the energy we breathe in, first *internally*, through the body; into the hands, the feet, and head, like a five-pointed star. I encourage clients to "feel energy flowing to you and through you." The idea is to feel powerful.

   You can also direct your energy *externally*, into whatever you are working to achieve.

This simple, powerful exercise can become a valuable habit for both recharging and preparing to deal with stressful situations. It is also a way to manage emotions. As stated, people tend to perform under pressure as they have previously performed under pressure in the past UNLESS they over train themselves to have control at a lower level of emotional intensity. In other words, to break a habit of feeling tense under pressure, practice creating feelings of ease in low-arousal, non-challenging situations. This can be accomplished by practicing relaxed, rhythmical breathing for a few minutes every day in non-threatening situations. Over time, the new feelings of ease and power generated by the breathing process will become firmly established in your behavioral repertoire. As they do, you will be able to experience a greater sense of ease and power going into pressure situations, and both confidence and performance will improve.

This is clearly an individual exercise and it's one that builds calm, confidence, and power. I found that it contributes to being a more effective performer and teammate. I have encouraged individuals and teams to do at least five to ten minutes of conscious breathing *every day*. From a team perspective it nurtures clarity, calm, and improved communication.

9. **The Power of the Circle:** Last, there are several team-building exercises that can be done with the team in a circle that strengthen team identity and harmony.

Exclusivity: A simple circle exercise that can be done in a few minutes is to have the team form a tight circle, facing outward with hands and arms firmly joined. One individual, preferably someone not a member of the team (e.g., I have often assumed this role as a consultant) is outside the circle. The group is instructed to keep the outsider out, not to let him or her into their circle. The outsider is told to try to penetrate the circle.

The jostling that ensues may be very active or less so, depending on the composition of the group. But the simple process illustrates and provides the group with an experience of exclusivity that in part defines their identity.

Support: Another simple circle exercise, and a variant of the exclusivity exercise above, is to have the team join hands and form a tight, small circle, facing inwards, with one team member positioned in the center of the circle. The person inside the circle holds his or her body stiffly (arms at sides) and allows him or herself to be gently moved in a supportive way around the inside of the circle. The team member in the center can feel the strength and support of the group as he or she is moved around the circle, and the team can experience themselves as a strong support system for all team members.

(There are other non-circular variations of the trust exercise that I have used successfully, like the trust fall, where an individual allows him or herself to fall backwards into the supportive hands of one or more attentive teammates.)

Energy: One exercise that I have found to be energizing that brings the group together is to have the group stand in a circle facing inwards with considerable space between each other and do a martial art punching and yelling drill. The sound or yell that accompanies the punch is called a *kiai* and is alleged to have evolved from a battle cry used to raise the fighting spirit of a troop.

First, group members gather in a spacious circle, flex their knees, and tune into their breathing. Then, all team members synchronize their breathing rhythm. On a count they begin punching gently (to start) at the air, at waist level, with alternative hands . . . as they exhale. After six to eight soft alternate hand punches to coordinate a team rhythm, eight to ten strong punches follow while emitting a deep loud "kiai" yell with each punch (and exhalation).

I have used the exercise with numerous sport teams prior to a match or to raise energy following a break in the action. I have also used it with business groups who have been sitting too long and need an energy boost. The effect has consistently been to raise the energy of the group, bring team members closer together, generate a good feeling, and ready the team to perform.

The supervisor of one factory team I worked with was a fan of the *haka*. The *haka* is a traditional stylized movement form of the Maori of New Zealand. Originally a group posture dance with shouted accompaniment, it has been popularized as an energizing pre-game ritual of New Zealand's All Blacks rugby team. The plant supervisor asked if there was some way we could bring the energy of the *haka* to the work teams. When we performed the circle punching exercise described above with team leaders and lead hands, the leadership group was very responsive. From time to time they are using the exercise to energize their work crews.

Harmony: A team-building circle exercise that is ostensibly an extension of the personal power exercise mentioned above, and one that's akin to meditation, is to have team members sit quietly in a circle, close their eyes, and tune into their breathing. They are specifically directed to focus on their breathing rhythm . . . and then bring to mind a single *silent* thought or sound (e.g., the sound can be "one"). They are directed to experience this process together, for a period of five to ten minutes. This group exercise builds composure and harmony and is especially effective leading up to and through an intense or stressful period (playoff, tournament, campaign), especially when the group is in unfamiliar territory. It can also be used as a retreat exercise to bring the group together.

This exercise is applicable to all teams. I recall working with a national team at a major international tournament in Venezuela. We were being housed in a building that was neither completely finished nor furnished, and was situated in some very noisy surroundings. At the end of our daily team meetings the team was directed to sit quietly in a circle, for five minutes, focusing on breathing and the thought "One." We even spent two minutes in the dressing room prior to games collectively getting composed.

As with all of these supportive exercises, there was some initial skepticism about the process by a few individuals when it was first introduced, but after a few days of practice, everyone settled into a quiet, positive sense of calm. Thereafter, little seemed to bother us, including the surroundings, the noise, transportation issues, or changes in schedule. We were calm, we were focused, and we won the gold medal.

Doing It

Several leaders I spoke with wanted to go on record to say that simply reading a book about why teams win was not going to make a significant difference in team performance—unless you actually implement the recommendations and lessons described in the book. One executive said, "There are a number of books written about success. But if you don't actively apply the advice in these books it's unlikely that it's going to have much impact on your performance."

I agree. Just reading about what makes a successful individual or a winning team isn't good enough. It's *doing it* that counts! Winning is about creating a goal, committing to doing *all* of what's necessary to achieve it, and then working together to make it happen.

Working with others and being part of a winning team in a highly competitive world is an opportunity, a challenge, and a joy.

I wish you great success and enjoyment in your endeavors.

REFERENCES

Introduction

1. Vince Lombardi, in *Iacocca: An Autobiograph*, Lee Iacocca with William Novak, Bantam Books, New York, 1984.

2. Helen Keller, *The Edge*, Howard Ferguson, Getting The Edge Co. Cleveland, OH, 1990.

3. Ken Wilber, *A Brief History of Everything*, Shambhala Publications, Inc., Boston, 1996.

4. Lorenzo Neal, radio interview, 2007.

5. Davey Johnson, personal communication.

6. Steve Ballmer, "What Makes A Winner," *BusinessWeek*, August 21/28, 2006.

7. Charlie Weis, in *No Excuses*, Charlie Weis and Vic Carrucci, Harper Collins, New York, 2006.

Chapter One

1. Stephen Covey, *The 7 Habits of Highly Successful People*, Simon & Schuster, New York, 1989.

2. Dick Irvin, personal communication.

3. Jeffery K. Liker, *The Toyota Way: 14 Management Principles from the World's Greatest Manufacturer*, McGraw-Hill, New York, 2004.

4. Charlie Weis, in *No Excuses*, Charlie Weis and Vic Carrucci, Harper Collins, New York, 2006.

Chapter Two

1. John Madden in *The Edge*, Howard Ferguson, Getting The Edge Co. Cleveland, OH, 1990.

2. Meredith Belbin, *Management Teams: Why They Succeed or Fail*, Butterworth-Heinemann, Oxford, 2000.

3. Rich Kromm, personal communication.

4. Andrew Carnegie in *The Edge*, Howard Ferguson, Getting The Edge Co. Cleveland, OH, 1990.

5. *Good To Great: Why Some Companies Make the Leap . . . and Others Don't*, Jim Collins, Harper Collins, New York, 2001.

6. Jim Collins, in "Collins on Tough Calls," *Fortune*, June 27, 2005.

7. Ken Holland in "The Motor City Method: The Red Wings' GM Shares Detroit's Nine Secrets to Stanley Cup Success," *The Hockey News*, July 1, 2008.

8. Michael Jordan.

9. Lanny Basham, *With Winning in Mind*, Book Partners, Wilsonville, OR, 1995.

10. Tiger Woods, ESPN Radio interview, 2008.

11. Rick Lanz, personal communication.

Chapter Three

1. Dave Dombrowski, Team Radio interview, 2007.

2. *Russell Rules*, Bill Russell with David Falkner, New American Library, New York, 2002.

3. Eric Wright, Team Radio interview, 2007.

4. Bill Walker, personal communication.

5. Joe Namath in *The Edge*, Howard Ferguson, Getting The Edge Co. Cleveland, OH, 1990.

6. Larry Huras, personal communication.

7. Tom Landry in *The Edge*, Howard Ferguson, Getting The Edge Co. Cleveland, OH, 1990.

8. John C. Maxwell, *The 360 Degree Leader*, Nelson Business/Thomas Nelson Publishers, Nashville, TN, 2005.

9. Ken Hitchcock, personal communication.

10. Doug Risebrough, personal communication.

11. Steve Yzerman, personal communication.

12. *Servant Leadership: A Journey into the Nature of Legitimate Power and Greatness*, 25th Anniversary Edition, Robert K. Greenleaf, edited by Larry C. Spears, Paulist Press, Manuah, NJ, 2002.

13. Jack Zenger, in "Position vs. Contribution: How Some People Lead Without a Title" *Leadership Excellence*, May 16, 2008.

14. Gord Huston, personal communication.

15. Casey Stengel in *The Edge*, Howard Ferguson, Getting The Edge Co. Cleveland, OH, 1990.

16. Darby Hendrickson, in *Hockey Tough: A Winning Mental Game*, Saul L. Miller, Human Kinetics, Champaign, Illinois, 2003.

Chapter Four

1. Bill Gates.

2. Branch Rickey, Baseball Quotations.

3. Lee Iacocca with William Novak, *Iacocca: An Autobiography*, Bantam Books, New York, 1984.

4. Even Pellerud, personal communication.

5. Steve Kerr, in "Risky Business: The New Pay Game," *Fortune*, July 22, 1996

6. Jim Collins, *Good to Great: Why Some Companies Make the Leap and Others Don't*, Harper Business: New York, 2001.

7. Daniel LaMarre, in "What Makes a Winner," *BusinessWeek*, August 21/28, 2006

8. Alan Brahmst, personal communication.

9. Bob Lutz in "Comin' Through!" Keith Naughton and Allan Sloan, *Newsweek* (Web Exclusive), 2007.

10. Jeffery Liker, *The Toyota Way: 14 Management Principals from the World's Greatest Manufacture*, Simon and Schuster, New York, 2004.

11. Merlin Olsen, *The Edge*, Howard Ferguson, Getting The Edge Co., Cleveland, OH, 1990.

Chapter Five

1. Gene Kranz, *Apollo 13*, *Failure I Not an Option: Mission Control from Mercury to Apollo and Beyond*, Berkley Books, New York, 2000.

2. Mark Jenkins, Ken Pasternak, Richard West, *Performance at the Limit: Business Lessons from Formula 1 Motor Racing*, Cambridge University Press, Cambridge, 2005.

3. Forrest Gregg in *The Edge*, Howard Ferguson, Getting The Edge Co., Cleveland, OH, 1990.

4. Gene Kranz, *Failure Is Not an Option: Mission Control from Mercury to Apollo and Beyond*, Berkley Books, New York, 2000.

5. David Wolfe, personal communication.

6. Wayne Gretzky.

7. Lee Iacocca with William Novak, *Iacocca: An Autobiography*, Bantam Books, New York, 1984.

8. Lou Holz, *Winning Every Day*, Harper Business Books, New York, 1998.

9. Lisa Endlich, *Goldman Sachs: The Culture of Success*, Knopf, New York, 1999.

10. Kevin Constantine, personal communication.

11. Vic Rapp, personal communication.

12. Mark Jenkins, Ken Pasternak, Richard West, *Performance at the Limit: Business Lessons from Formula 1 Motor Racing*, Cambridge University Press, Cambridge, 2005.

13. Henry Mintzberg, personal communication.

14. Calvin Coolidge in *The Edge*, Howard Ferguson, Getting The Edge Co., Cleveland, OH, 1990.

15. Bobby Knight in *The Edge*, Howard Ferguson, Getting The Edge Co., Cleveland, OH, 1990.

16. Vince Lombardi in *The Edge*, Howard Ferguson, Getting The Edge Co., Cleveland, OH, 1990.

17. Forrest Gregg in *The Edge*, Howard Ferguson, Getting The Edge Co., Cleveland, OH, 1990.

18. Roger Neilson, personal communication.

Chapter Six

1. David Thielen, *The 12 Simple Secrets of Microsoft Management*, McGraw Hill, New York, 1999.

2. Dan Allen, personal communication.

3. Tom Webster, personal communication.

4. Dave "Tiger" Williams, personal communication.

5. Ken Blanchard and Spencer Johnson, *The One-Minute Manager*, Berkley Books, New York, 1981.

6. Cliff Ronning, personal communication.

7. Daniel Goleman, in "What Makes a Leader," *Harvard Business Review*, Nov.–Dec. 1998.

8. Roger Neilson, personal communication.

9. Arnold Glasgow in *The Edge*, Howard Ferguson, Getting The Edge Co., Cleveland, OH, 1990.

10. Bill Russell with David Falkner, *Russell Rules*, New American Library, New York, 2002.

11. Cleve Backster, *Primary Perception: Biocommunication with plants, living foods, and human cells*, White Rose Millennium Press, 2003.

Chapter Seven

1. Y.A. Tittle in *The Edge*, Howard Ferguson, Getting The Edge Co. Cleveland, OH, 1990.

2. Vince Lombardi in *The Edge*, Howard Ferguson, Getting The Edge Co., Cleveland, OH, 1990.

3. Bobby Knight in *The Edge*, Howard Ferguson, Getting The Edge Co. Cleveland, OH, 1990.

4. Roger Staubach in *The Edge*, Howard Ferguson, Getting The Edge Co. Cleveland, OH, 1990.

5. Mark Jenkins, Ken Pasternak, Richard West, *Performance at the Limit: Business Lessons from Formula 1 Motor Racing*, Cambridge University Press, Cambridge, 2005.

6. Richard Church, personal communication.

7. Don Shula and Ken Blanchard, *Everyone's a Coach*, Harper Business, New York, 1995.

8. Bill Parcells with Jeff Coplon in *Parcells: Finding a Way to Win*, Doubleday, New York, 1995.

9. Phil Jackson, *Sacred Hoops: Spiritual Lessons of a Hardwood Warrior*, Hyperion, New York, 1995.

Chapter Eight

1. Lee Iacocca with William Novak, *Iacocca: An Autobiography*, Bantam Books, New York, 1984.

2. Scott Mellanby, personal communication.

3. Mark Messier, personal communication.

4. Davey Johnson, personal communication.

5. Nadira Laing, personal communication.

6. Mark Jenkins, Ken Pasternak, Richard West, *Performance at the Limit: Business Lessons from Formula 1 Motor Racing*, Cambridge University Press, Cambridge, 2005.

7. *Miracle*, film directed by Gavin O'Connor, 2004.

8. Lloyd Jones, *The Book of Fame*, Penguin Books, New Zealand, 2000.

9. Bret Hedican, personal communication.

10. Martha K. McClintock, "The McClintock Effect," *Nature*, 1971.

11. Bruce Coslett in *The Edge*, Howard Ferguson, Getting The Edge Co., Cleveland, OH, 1990.

12. Bill Bradley, *Values of the Game*, Artisan, New York, 1998.

13. Danny Ainge, radio interview, 2008.

14. Rudyard Kipling, "The Law of the Jungle," *The Jungle Book*.

Chapter Nine

1. Scotty Bowman, personal communication.

2. Doug Reisborough, personal communication.

Chapter Ten

1. Craig Channell, personal communication.

2. John Wooden, *Wooden: A Lifetime of Observations and Reflections On and Off the Court*, Contemporary, Lincolnwood, IL, 1997.

3. Robert Dirk, personal communication.

4. Satoshi Hino, *Inside the Mind of Toyota*, Productivity Press, New York, 2006.

5. Jeffery K. Liker, personal communication, 2008.

6. Satoshi Hino, *Inside the Mind of Toyota*, Productivity Press, New York, 2006.

7. Jeffery K Liker and David P Meier, *Toyota Talent: Developing Your People the Toyota Way*, McGraw Hill 2007.

8. Jeffery K. Liker, *The Toyota Way*, Simon and Schuster, New York, 2004.

9. Hirotaka Takeuchi, Emi Osono, and Norihiko Shimizu, "The Contradictions That Drive, Toyota's Success," *The Harvard Business Review*, June 2000.

10. Hirotaka Takeuchi, Emi Osono, and Norihiko Shimizu, "The Contradictions That Drive, Toyota's Success," *The Harvard Business Review*, June 2000.

11. "Comin' Through!" by Keith Naughton and Allan Sloan, *Newsweek* Web Exclusive.

12. Jack Welch quoted in an interview with Nikkei Sangyo Shimbum, November, 2001.

13. Jeffery K. Liker, personal communication, 2008.

14. Jeffery K. Liker, *The Toyota Way*, Simon and Schuster, New York, 2004.

15. Tiger Woods, ESPN radio interview, 2008.

16. Jeffery K. Liker, personal communication, 2008.

17. "Comin' Through!" by Keith Naughton and Allan Sloan, *Newsweek* Web Exclusive.

18. Jeffery K. Liker, personal communication, 2008.

19. Teruyuki Minoura, Address given at 2003 Automotive Parts System Solution Fair, Tokyo, June 18, 2003.

20. Pat Riley in *The Winner Within: A Life Plan for Team Players*, Berkley Books, New York, 1993.

21. Jeffery K. Liker, personal communication, 2008.

Chapter Eleven

1. Robert Keidel, *Game Plans: Sport Strategies for Business.*

2. Roger Neilson, personal communication.

3. Davey Johnson, personal communication.

4. Bruce Tuckman, "Team Development Model, Developmental Sequence in Small Groups," *Psychological Bulletin*, 63, 384–399.

5. Gord Huston, personal communication.

Chapter Twelve

1. *Far Side* cartoon by Gary Larsen.

2. Saul L. Miller, *Hockey Tough: A Winning Mental Game*, Human Kinetics, Champaign, Illinois, 2003.

3. Adapted from Jeff Janssen, *The Team Captain's Leadership Manual*, Winning The Mental Game, Cary, North Carolina, 2007.

4. Dan Allen, personal communication.

BIBLIOGRAPHY

Books

A Brief History of Everything, Ken Wilber, Shambhala Publications, Inc., Boston, 1996.

Baseball Quotations, edited by David H. Nathan, Ballantyne Books, New York, 1990.

Everyone's a Coach, Don Shula & Ken Blanchard, Harper Business, New York, 1995.

Failure Is Not an Option: Mission Control from Mercury to Apollo and Beyond, Gene Kranz, Berkley Books, New York, 2000.

Game Plans: Sport Strategies for Business, Robert W. Keidel, Berkley Books, New York, 1986.

Goldman Sachs: The Culture of Success, Lisa J. Endlich, Knopf, New York, 1999.

Good to Great: Why Some Companies Make the Leap and Others Don't, Jim Collins, Harper Collins, New York, 2001.

Hockey Tough: A Winning Mental Game, Saul L. Miller, Human Kinetics, Champaign, Illinois, 2003.

Iacocca: An Autobiography, Lee Iacocca with William Novak, Bantam Books, New York, 1984.

Management Teams: Why They Succeed or Fail, Meredith Belbin, Butterworth-Heinemann, Oxford, 2000.

No Excuses, Charlie Weis and Vic Carrucci, Harper Collins, New York , 2006.

Parcells: Finding a Way to Win: The Principles of Leadership, Teamwork, and Motivation, Bill Parcells with Jeff Coplon, Doubleday, New York, 1995.

Performance at the Limit: Business Lessons From Formula 1 Motor Racing, Mark Jenkins, Ken Pasternak, Richard West, Cambridge University Press, Cambridge, 2005.

Primary Perception: Biocommunication with Plants, Living Foods, and Human Cells, Cleve Backster, White Rose Millennium Press, 2003.

Russell Rules, Bill Russell with David Falkner, New American Library, New York, 2002.

Sacred Hoops: Spiritual Lessons of a Hardwood Warrior, Phil Jackson, Hyperion, New York, 1995.

The Book of Fame, Lloyd Jones, Penguin Books, New Zealand, 2000.

The Edge, Howard Ferguson, Getting The Edge Co. Cleveland, OH, 1990.

The One-Minute Manager, Ken Blanchard, Spencer Johnson. Berkley Books, New York, 1981.

The One-Minute Manager Builds High-Performance Teams, Ken Blanchard, Donald Carew, Eunice Parisi-Carew, William Morrow & Co., New York, 1990.

The 360 Degree Leader, John C. Maxwell, Nelson Business/Thomas Nelson Publishers, Nashville, TN, 2005.

Servant Leadership: A Journey Into the Nature of Legitimate Power and Greatness, 25th Anniversary Edition, Robert K. Greenleaf, edited by Larry C. Spears, forward by Stephen R. Covey, afterword by Peter Senge, Paulist Press, Manuah, NJ, 2002.

The 7 Habits of Highly Successful People, Stephen Covey, Simon and Schuster, New York, 1989.

The 12 Simple Secrets of Microsoft Management, David Thielen, McGraw Hill, New York, 1999.

The Team Captain's Leadership Manual, Jeff Janssen, Winning the Mental Game, Cary, NC, 2001.

Toyota Culture: The Heart and Soul of the Toyota Way, Jeffery Liker and Michael Hoseus, McGraw Hill, New York, 2008.

Toyota Talent: Developing Your People the Toyota Way, Jeffery Liker and David Meier, McGraw Hill, 2007.

The Toyota Way: 14 Management Principles from the World's Greatest Manufacturer Jeffrey Liker, McGraw Hill, New York, 2004.

The Winner Within, Pat Riley, Berkley Books, New York, 1993.

Values of the Game, Bill Bradley, Artisan, New York, 1998.

Winning Every Day, Lou Holz, Harper Business Books, New York, 1998.

With Winning in Mind, Lanny Basham, Book Partners, Wilsonville, OR, 1995.

Wooden: A Lifetime of Observations and Reflections On and Off the Court, John Wooden with Steve Jamison, Contemporary Books, Lincolnwood, IL, 1997.

Periodicals/Magazines

BusinessWeek, "What Makes a Winner," August 21/28, 2006.

Fortune, "Collins on Tough Calls," June 27, 2005.

The Excellence Issue—What It Takes to Be Great, October 30, 2006.

Fortune, "Risky Business: The New Pay Game—GE's Pay System Gets People Working Faster and Smarter," Steve Kerr, July 22, 1996.

Harvard Business Review, "The Contradictions That Drive Toyota's Success," Hirotaka Takeuchi, Emi Osono, and Norihiko Shimizu, June, 2008.

Harvard Business Review, "What Makes A Leader?" Daniel Golman, November-December, 1998.

Hockey News, "Ken Holland: The Motor City Method: The Red Wings' GM Shares Detroit's Nine Secrets to Stanley Cup Success," July 1, 2008.

Leadership Excellence, "Position vs. Contribution: How Some People Lead Without a Title," Jack Zenger, May 16, 2008.

Newsweek, "Comin" Through! Toyota Is on Track to Pass General Motors This Year as the World's No. 1 Auto Company," Keith Naughton and Allan Sloan, (Web Exclusive), 2007.

Psychological Bulletin, "Developmental Sequence in Small Groups," Bruce Tuckman.

INDEX

The symbol "§" indicates epigraph, at chapter beginnings or in text.

A

ABCs
  for breathing, 99, 101
  and captain's groups, 166
  for success, 57, 58
ability to motivate, 36
absenteeism (Toyota), 154
accomplishment, 82
accountability, 84–86
achievement, 16
acknowledgement, 77,
  86, 93
action, and vision, 57
adapting (game plan), 53
affirmations, 124
Ainge, Danny, 114
anger (coach), 40
animals
  as team, 5
  v. angels, 115

anxiety, 99, 100
Apollo 13, 61
assembly line, 158
assessment, 77
atoms and magnets,
  131–132
attention to detail, 35
attitude
  and perseverance, 72
  v. skill, 27, 147
audible-ready, 102
Auerbach, Red, 35
awareness development
  team-building, 169

B

Backster, Cleve, 93
balance, and commitment, 74
Ballmer, Steve, 7
baseball, 70, 161–162

Bashman, Lanny, 30

basketball

as flow game, 104, 159, 160

as horizontal game, 52

and individualism, 113

player blend, 66

and team members, 28

Belbin, R. Meredith, 26

Blanchard, Ken, 86

body, as core quality,
     133–134

The Book of Fame, 112

bottom line, 8, 78

Bowman, Scotty, 119§

Bradley, Bill, 113

Brahmst, Alan, 52

breathing

ABCs, 101

conscious, 100–102

and control, 99

and creating ease, 55

before event, 123

exercises, 183–185, 186

and love, 122

A Brief History of Everything,
     5

Brooks, Herb, 111

Bryant, Kobe, 43

Burying the Past (exercise),
     179–180

bus (exercise), 175–176

business

accountability, 84

bottom line, 78

and buying in, 66

captains, 42–43

and commitment, 61–62

competition, 109

game plan, 52

and health, 98

leaders, 38–39

plan, 158

special coaching for, 157–167

and sports, 8–9

and success, 50

and team success, 22

C

Campany, Michael, 71

captains, 42

"captain's groups," 43, 165–167,
     176

Carbonneau, Guy, 42

care, defined, 16

car manufacturers, 53–54

Carnegie, Andrew, 28

car ratings, 152

cephalo-caudal principle, 33

Chapman, Annemarie, 27

character, defined, 131

chemistry

and commitment, 68

and competition, 109
good, 107
and heart, 112
and leadership training, 143
and respect/love, 107–108
as social climate, 142
as team culture, 143
and team success, 63
at Toyota, 152–153
and trust, 109
and winning, 117
chie, 147
chimps, 114–115
Cirque du Soliel, 51
cliques, 142, 143
COACH, 102–103
coach
    and motivation, 19–20, 36
    and personal success, 36
    treatment of team, 40
coaching
    baseball, 161–162
    described, 39–40
    for different teams, 137, 157–158
    styles, 9
    as up-and-down process, 47
    video, 139
collaborating, 111
collective attitude, 64
collective peer feedback
        (exercise), 172–174

Collins, Jim, 29, 51
command (control), 98
commitment
    and balance, 74
    and corporate identity,
        68
    defined, 74
    described, 133
    and discipline, 71
    exercise, 177
    and goal, 60
    lack of, 64–65
    at Microsoft, 81–82
    team, and gravitational effect,
        60
    as team requirement, 5
    and team success, 63
    as top-down, 139–140
    and trust, 110
    and winning, 73–75
commitment (Toyota),
        149–150
communication
    and leadership, 34–35
    styles, 39
competition, 7, 109
competitiveness, 78
"competitive strategy," 51
complacency as enemy (Toyota),
        151
composure, exercise, 177

compromise, 68

confidence
  for different teams,
    141–142
  exercise, 177
  Toyota, 151
  word origin, 102

conscious breathing,
  100–102

consistency, 102, 139

Constantine, Kevin, 3

Consumer Reports, 152

continuous improvement, 8–9,
  150, 151

contraction, 55

control (command), 98

conviction, 102

Coolidge, Calvin, 72

core leadership, 50

corporate
  identity, 68
  transformation, 61

Coslett, Bruce, 113§

Covey, Stephen, 16

culture
  at Goldman Sachs, 65
  improving, 137, 138, 169
  no-blame, 111
  and recruiting, 27
  and team-building, 140, 143
  at Toyota, 143

D

daily metrics (Toyota), 151

decisions (who *v.* what), 29–30

degree, and commitment, 63–64

Design Group Staffing, 27

Desjardins, Will, 21

development of species, 163

Dickerson, Eric, 38

discipline, 71, 73–75

dis-ease, 55, 99

Dixon, George, 112

Dombrowski, Dave, 34–35

dopamine, 2

Drucker, Peter, 157§

Dryden, Ken, 21

E

Edsel, 78

effective communication, 91

ego, 60

emotion, 72, 98–99

emotional control, 40

empathy, 91

employee responsibility (Toyota),
  149–150

Endlich, Lisa, 65

energy, 8, 186–187

environmental issues, 20

Envision Financial, 3

evaluation process, 79

evolution, 5–6

excellence, and pressure, 152
exclusivity (exercise), 185–186
exercises, 170–188
extroversion types, 45

F
factories, 158
failure, 61–62
family values, 178
fear, 121–122
feedback, 140–141
    and captain's groups, 165–166
    exercise, 172–174, 177
    negative, 89
    and performance, 80
    positive, 88, 89
    and progress, 80
    and success measures, 141
    at Toyota, 150–151
    in training camp, 87–88
"feeling right," 98–99
feeling types, 39, 45
flow, and chemistry, 153
"flow games," 28, 52, 104,
       159–161. See also baseball,
    basketball, soccer
focus
    and leadership, 34
    and performance, 56
    and perseverance, 72
    style, 46

and success, 50
and winning, 74
football, 52–53, 158–159
Ford, Henry, 169§
forming stage (teams), 163
Formula 1 racing, 69, 97

G
game of the plan, 52, 158–159
game plan, 53–54, 67, 148–149
*Game Plans: Sport Strategies for
    Business*, 158
Gates, Bill, 49§, 145, 149
geese (logo exercise), 175
General Motors, 53–54, 111
get the job done, 29, 74, 139
Glasgow, Arnold, 92§
goals
    defined, 16
    effects of, 15–16
    realizing, 60
    and teamwork, 111
    winning *v.* losing, 135–136
Goldman Sachs, 65, 82
*Goldman Sachs, The Culture of
    Success*, 65
Goleman, Daniel, 91
golf, as "I" game, 121
Good to Great, 29, 51
gravitational effect, 60
Gregg, Forest, 59§, 74

Gretzky, Wayne, 62
group activities, 169–188
group identity, 178

H

haka, 187
harmony, 27, 68, 113
harmony (exercise), 185, 187–188
Hatcher, Derian, 42
head leads, body follows, 33, 47,
    127, 137, 148
health
    and confidence, 97–98
    and desire to excel, 15
    and motivation, 18
health care costs, 54
Hedican, Bret, 112
Hendrickson, Darby, 47
Hino, Satoshi, 146
hiring process, Toyota, 147
Hitchcock, Ken, 41–42
hockey, 52, 66, 157, 159–160
*Hockey Tough: A Winning Mental
    Game*, 2, 175
Holland, Ken, 30
Holz, Lou, 64
honesty, 102
horizontal organization, 80, 159
hoshin kanri, 145, 149
Hull, Brett, 42
humility (Toyota), 151, 154

Huras, Larry, 39–40
Huston, Gord, 3, 44, 167
hybrid vehicles, 148

I

identifying talent, 26
identity
    as self-image, 119
    and team-building, 143–144
    Toyota, 154–155
    and winning teams, 120
"I" games, 121, 161, 162
imaginary survival scenarios, 169
improvement, continual, 86
individual, developing, 163
innovation (Toyota), 148
Inside the Mind of Toyota, 146
insight exercises, 170–188
intelligence, 8, 26, 27–28
intention, 133
interdisciplinary clinic, 45, 53,
    69, 79–80, 120
introversion types, 45
intuitive types, 45
Irvin, Dick, 21
"I" v. "we," 60, 65, 70, 110, 121,
    134, 139, 161, 162

J

Jackson, Phil, 104
JD Power survey, 151

Jenkins, Mark, 111
job security (Toyota), 153
Johnson, Davey, 7, 108–109, 110
Jones, Lloyd, 112
Jordan, Michael, 30, 43, 104
J) types, 45

K
kaizen, 22, 146, 148, 151
kanri, 145
Keane, Mike, 42
Keidel, Robert, 158
Keller, Helen, 5§
Kerr, Steve, 50, 53
killer instinct, 39
Kipling, Rudyard, 116–117
Knight, Bob, 73, 96
know-how, 25
knowing the job, 50, 53, 56, 92, 96, 138
knowledge workers, 147
Kranz, Gene, 59§, 61
Kromm, Rich, 27–28

L
labeling, 92
labor agreements, 54
Lamarre, Daniel, 51
Landry, Tom, 40
Lanz, Rick, 31
lateral inhibitions, 74

law of the jungle, 115–117
leaders, 38–39
leadership
    ability to motivate, 36
    attention to detail, 35
    communication, 34–35
    core, 41–45
    described, 33–34
    effective, 37
    encouraging, 43
    exercise, 176–177
    focus, 34
    forms of, 41
    goals, 37–38
    nurturing, 41
    as organizing force, 33–34
    player response to, 66–67
    poor, 112
    and self-awareness, 91
    sports *v*. business, 70
    stages of development, 164–165
    strategy, 69
    styles, 9
    and talent, 69
    and team commitment, 69
    and team culture, 114
    and team success, 63
    timing, 162–165
    Toyota, 148
    and two teams, 137–138
    understanding, 47

the leadership brain, 33

the leadership ear, 33

the leadership eye, 33

Leadership for All (exercise), 176–177

the leadership voice, 33

learning, 39, 80

LeMond, Greg, 119–120

Leyland, Jim, 34–35

Liker, Jeffery K., 54, 145, 146, 147, 150, 151, 154

the "line," 159

locomotive, 175

Logo Exercise, 174–175

Lombardi, Vince, 4§, 50, 52, 64, 74, 96, 107, 169§

love, and fear, 121–122

luck, 49–50

Lutz, Bob, 148

M

Madden, John, 25§

making things, 153

Management Teams, 26

manufacturing, 158

Manulife Financial, 110–111

maturity, 25

Maxwell, John, 41§

the McClintock effect, 112

meaning, 15

meaninglessness, 17–19

measuring accountability, 84

"me first" times, 113

Meier, David, 146

Mellanby, Scott, 108

mental skills, 96

Messier, Mark, 95, 108

"me" *v.* "we," 28, 29, 64–65, 68, 117, 150

Microsoft, 81–83

mind, as core quality, 133

mind leads, body follows, 33, 47, 127, 137, 148

mindset, 26

Minouri, Teruyuki, 153

Mintzberg, Henry, 70

mission

and collective buy-in, 20

defining, 20–21

statement, 22

Modano, Mike, 42

modeling, 40, 67, 165, 166, 177

motivation, 16–17, 19–20, 28, 35, 42, 83, 131

Mullen, Joe, 42

Myers-Briggs Type Indicator, 39, 45

N

Namath, Joe, 36

Neal, Lorenzo, 6

negative eyes, 88

negative feedback, 89, 91

negative thinking, 122

Neilson, Roger, 74, 92, 159

Neuendyke, Joe, 42

nicknames, 122–123

Nike, 8–9

no-blame culture, 111

No Excuses, 8

norming stage (teams), 164

O

Olsen, Merlin, 56

Olympics, 2008, 60–61

The One Minute Manager, 86–87

ontogeny, 163

organizations, 80, 163

Osono, Emi, 147

Overcoming Inertia (exercise),
    175–176

over-learning, 102

P

Parcells, Bill, 103, 158

passing the puck, 159

Pasternak, Ken, 111

pay (Toyota), 154, 155

Pellerud, 50

people development, 163

performance

    and acknowledgement, 93

    bonuses, 69

and feedback, 80, 90

indicators, 78

measuring, 79

model, 86

v. seniority, 80

performance anxiety, 122, 125

*Performance at the Limit: Business
    Lessons from Formula 1 Motor
    Racing*, 111

performance-based incentives, 22

performing stage (teams), 164

perseverance, 71–73

personal action plan, 55–56

personal goal, 135

Personal Identity (exercise),
    180–183

personality styles, 39, 45

Personal Power (exercise),
    183–185

Person in the Middle (exercise),
    172

phylogeny, 163

physical skills, 96

plan, 49, 54

planning process, 52

plants, and praise, 93

player ego, 67–68

player-leaders, 41, 44

positive eyes, 87

positive feedback, 90

positive identity, 121

post-game feedback, 79

Power of the Circle (exercise), 185–188

power statement, 124–125

practice, 30–31

praise, 87

"pre-game plan," 56

preparation, 56, 95, 96, 104, 125

pressure, and excellence, 152

pride, 115

prioritizing, 34

problem-solving team-building, 169

production targets (Toyota), 149

profanity, and coach, 40

profitability, 20

progress, and feedback, 80

psycho-physical exercises, 71

P) types, 45

purpose

　and captain's groups, 166

　and collective buy-in, 20

R

Rapp, Vic, 67, 69

rating (performance), 79

reacting v. thinking, 103

recreational team-building, 169

recruiting talent, 26, 27

Reisborough, Doug, 42, 120

repetition, 103, 122

respect, 22

respect for people (Toyota), 151

respect for workers (Toyota), 149

response-ability, 19–20, 84, 122, 123, 165

responsibility, 84–86

　and coach, 36

　described, 84–85

　management, 42, 44, 104

　personal, 28, 29

　social, 20

　taking, 71

　and teams, 71

rhythmic breathing, 55

Rickey, Branch, 49

"right feeling," 98–99

right people on bus, 29, 30

Riley, Pat, 153–154§

Ronning, Cliff, 47

routine, 56

Russell, Bill, 35, 40, 92

Russell's Rules, 92

S

Sacred Hoops, 104

sales, as "I" game, 121, 162

sales teams, 70, 111

Sather, Glen, 21

scavenger hunts, 170

score, 77

scoreboard, 83, 86

scorecard, 78

scouting, 136–137

selective perception, 87

self-awareness, 91

self-belief, 142

self-control, and breathing, 100

self-rating (performance), 79

self-regulation, 91

"selling" the dream, 36

sense of purpose, 15, 18–19

sensory factual types, 45

servant leadership, 43, 150

shaping, 69, 87, 138–139, 140, 141

Shimizu, Norihiko, 147

Shorter Version (feedback exercise), 172–173

Shula, Don, 102, 103, 158

Singh, V.J., 121

skill

  and confidence, 96

  and practice, 96–97

  v. attitude, 27, 147

Skrudland, Brian, 42

SMART, 82

Snyder, Bruce, 38

soccer, 52, 158–159, 160

social responsibility, 20

"soul power," 15

specific success factors, 55

spirit, 8, 134

sport

  as model for business, 53

  as performance model, 3

sports, and business, 8–9

standards of excellence, 90

star player, 67–68

Staubach, Roger, 97

Stengel, Casey, 45

Stewart, Jackie, 59§, 69–70

storming stage (teams), 163

strategy, 63, 138–139

Strawberry, Darryl, 109

success

  ABCs for, 57

  acknowledging, 141

  and adjustment, 83

  and commitment, 63

  and confidence, 95

  as expectation, 120

  factors, 54, 78–79

  in flow games, 160

  how to measure, 78

  in marketing business, 160

  as measurement, 81

  measuring, 80

  mentality, 151

  as product of plan, 158–159

  and team culture, 114

superstar, 28

swearing, 90–91

sweat *v.* glory, 85

SWOT analysis, 52
synergy, 134, 159

T
Takeuchi, Hirotaka, 147
talent
  acquiring, 26–27
  and culture, 27
  developing, 26
  as fusion, 30
  identifying, 26–27
  and performance, 136–137
  and practice, 30–31
  psychological qualities of, 26
  recruiting, 26–27
  and responsibility, 28–29
  and scouting, 136–137
  and synergy, 8
  and team-building training,
    137
  and team success, 63
  as unit of weight, 25
targets (Toyota), 146
team
  as acronym, 7
  challenge, 5
  chemistry, 113
  as collection of individuals, 162
  defined, 4–5
  development of, 163
  exercises, 170–188

  as family, 128
  and functional family values,
    143
  goal, and personal goal, 135
  heartbeat, 112
  identity, 126–129
  as locomotive, 175
  meetings, 50–51, 52
  members, 15
  as organized group, 159
  relays, 169
  residences, 143
  retreat, 111
  role, defined, 26
  sales, 70
  special coaching for, 157–167
  success, and feedback, 77
  success, and individual agenda,
    135–136
  targets, 42
  and work ethic, 29
team-building, 169–188
*The Team Captain's Leadership
    Manual*, 176
Team Identity (exercise), 178–180
Team Reflection-Action
    (exercise), 170–172
teamwork, 28
technical skills, 96
tenderness, 40
tension, 99

Thielen, David, 81

thinking-feeling dimension, 39

thinking types, 39, 45

thinking v. reacting, 103

Thornton, Joe, 175

three360-degree exercise, 172–174

threesix360 reviews, 83

tiger, 114–115

timing, and leadership, 162–165

Tittle, Y.A., 96

top down commitment, 61

top down leadership, 50

toughness, 40

Toyota

coaching leaders, 43

employees, 146

as family, 152

goal-setting process, 145

hiring process, 147

leadership, 148

measuring success, 80

mission statement, 146

and purpose, 145–146

strategies, 54

targets, 146

training program, 147

and value for customers, 146

Toyota Management, 149

Toyota Motor Corporation, 145

Toyota Production System (TPS), 54, 149, 153

Toyota Talent, 146

The Toyota Way, 54

the Toyota Way, 22, 148

training

camps, 87–88

program (Toyota), 147

year-round, 6

trampoline, 60

trust

and chemistry, 109

in leadership, 69

and managers, 104

and teamwork, 111

The 360 Degree Leader, 41

Tuckman, Bruce, 163

turnover (Toyota), 154

The 12 Simple Secrets of Microsoft Management, 81

U

unions, 22, 150, 152

V

validity, 78

value, and team members, 15

"vehicles to avoid" list, 152

vertical leadership, 41, 47, 52, 158